D0623375

shells

PAUL STAROSTA | JACQUES SENDERS

shells

preface by Paolo Portoghesi

Rita and Jacques Senders Collection

FIREFLY BOOKS

Contents

From Nature to Architecture

Paolo Portoghesi

"The shelled nautilus," wrote Aristotle in his *Historia Animalium*, "rises up from deep water and swims on the surface; it rises with its shell down-turned in order that it may rise the more easily and swim with it empty, but after reaching the surface it shifts the position of the shell. In between its feelers it has a certain amount of web-growth, resembling the substance between the toes of web-footed birds; only that with these latter the substance is thick, while with the nautilus it is thin and like a spider's web. It uses this structure, when a breeze is blowing, for a sail, and lets down some of its feelers alongside as rudder-oars. If it be frightened it fills its shell with water and sinks." This legend was further expounded by Pliny the Elder in his *Naturalis Historia*, calling this mollusk the first "sailor" of the oceans. The second-century Greek poet Oppian attributed the power of flight to this mollusk in his ode, calling it a god: "Oh fish, so dear to sailors! Your presence signals the advent of gentle and friendly winds; you bring serenity and serve as its sign."

Today we know that *Argonauta*, as Linnaeus named the cephalopod first described by Aristotle, is in fact a separate genus of shellfish. The female carries a thin, incubating membrane filled with eggs behind her until it is emptied and left behind in the water. The fascinating illustration in Louis Figuier's book *La Vie et les moeurs des animaux* (1866) clearly illustrates the sail-like structure that gave rise to this misconception.

The direct link with the sea, and hence lunar cycles and femininity, as well as the association with sound and the ear, account for the extraordinary symbolism connected with the shells of various mollusk families and species. It should be noted that shells can be observed and studied from two very different perspectives. They can simply be seen as empty containers to be collected and admired, or they can be studied in detail as parts of complex living organisms whose morphology, ways of life and interactions have been shaped by their environment. The first approach, based on detailed knowledge of classification, is known as chonchology. Malacology, the wider, more scientific approach, is a branch of zoology that studies all mollusks including, for example, cuttlefish, which have a kind of flattened internal shell, as immortalized in Eugenio Montale's poem "*Ossi di sepia.*"

This rather odd situation has prompted questions as to the relationship between shells and the animals that live inside them. One old metaphor, echoed by Leonardo da Vinci, is that the mollusk shell is like a house. A real house, however, is not just used for shelter and protection; it is also something that we can leave as we wish. In other words, the value of a house is not just that we can enter and leave it at will, but also that it serves as an individual's home, and a center of familiar surroundings. A shell, on the other hand, is more like a prison, with only one exterior opening, allowing the animal to extend outward but not leave it completely. Another metaphor compares it to a skeleton, although a shell is really just an external skeleton. Unlike our own internal skeleton, well hidden under skin

The Argonaut mollusk that navigates the high seas, in Louis Figuier's *The Life and Death of Animals: Zoophytes and Mollusks*, Paris, 1866.

and flesh, which gives us body shape and support, the skeleton of mollusks is strictly external, a protective coat that is attached to the animal's body by a membranous mantle. This strictly scientific definition of a skeleton is useful for classification purposes, but understates the important and very complex link between the shell and the animal living within it. While the vertebrate skeleton is a basic component that grows along with an organism's other tissues and is only indirectly evident from the outside, the mollusk's shell is the animal's most visible feature.

In a sense, a shell is like a sculpture atop a platform — in this case the mollusk. However, while most platforms are simple geometric structures not intended to compete with the artwork they support, the situation is entirely the reverse in mollusks. The platform, in this case the body of the organism, is a flexible, organic entity that changes shape constantly. Shells, on the other hand, are complex, geometric structures that combine two characteristics — harmony and competition — as shown by the diversity of colors and surface patterns. As Pliny observed in this context: *magna ludentis naturae varietas* ("this contrasting glitter expresses the great variety of nature at play").

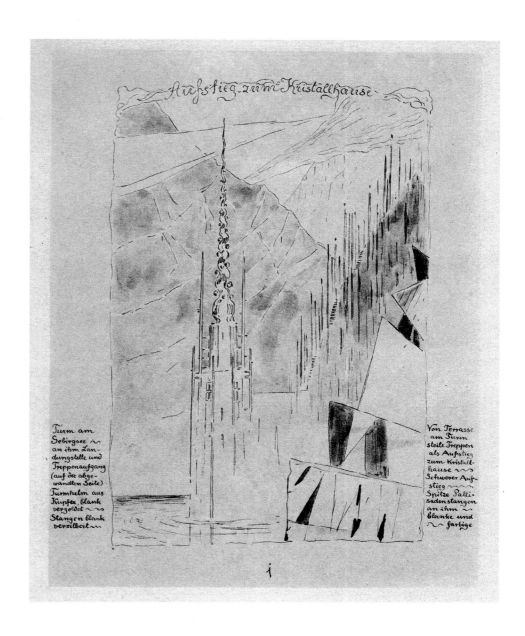

It was Archimedes who first identified the laws that determine the formation of the spiral that carries his name, which is like a rope wound around itself. This shape is very similar to that typical of ammonites, fossil mollusks with a spiral shell, which have been extinct for millions of years but have always been of great interest to naturalists. The difference, however, is that shell spirals are not constant in size because they gradually grow in thickness. In the 16th century, at the beginning of the baroque art form, the great philosopher Descartes defined an equiangular (equal-angled) spiral which, when wound in three dimensions, characterized the shells of gastropods. At the same time in Rome, the cauldron of baroque art, a passion for shells arose in the newly founded Accademia dei Lincei, and were pictured in *Le Stanze delle Meraviglie* by Simone Martini to Francesco Mochi, as well as in precious books like Jesuit Filippo Bonanni's *Ricreazione dell'occhio e della mente nell'osservazione delle chiocciole*, which shows some 450 diverse species of shells.

It fell, however, to a great architect, Christopher Wren (1632–1723), professor of astronomy at age 25 and the builder of St. Paul's Cathedral in London, to discover a direct link between shells and the equiangular or trigonometric spiral. Architect Thomas Wallis states that Wren saw the shape of a shell as a cone turned around its axis, and that the resulting spiral's angle was unique for each animal species. The extraordinary mathematical properties of the Cartesian spiral were of particular

Emilio Terry, a snail house project, c. 1930.

interest. Mathematician James Bernoulli referred to it as *spira mirabilis* ("the marvelous spiral") and wanted to adorn his tomb with it, because the ratio of its length to its width remains constant, causing it to steadily curve outward toward infinity. "This marvelous spiral," he wrote, "pleases me greatly because of its unique and admirable properties, which I have difficulty erasing from my mind." The discovery of the *spira mirabilis* mathematical regularity in the structure of shells, particularly in planar sections of *Nautilus pompilius*, was confirmed in the early 1800s in scientific terms by Canon Moseley. This was subsequently extended to various other species by Theodore Cook in *The Curves of Life* (1914) and by D'Arcy Wentworth Thompson in his famous book *On Growth and Form* (1917), where he shows the use of the ancient concept of the gnomon to explain shell growth modes. Gnomon is an ancient Greek term meaning "indicator" — a vertical L-shaped pointer or the square used by a bricklayer to help maintain the level of a rising structure. The same approach had been applied by Erone of Alexandria to all types of surfaces that basically have similar characteristics. When the outlines of mollusk shells are projected onto a level plane, their starting components meet at a central nucleus that is similar to a gnomon. Often as well, these components are clearly distinguishable from each other by external demarcation lines or, as in *Nautilus* species, by a succession of chambers. The largest and youngest of these chambers houses the animal, while the rest are filled with air for ballast to regulate descent and ascent in the water.

This type of growth mode fundamentally differs from that seen in the human body. When a person grows, his or her hands increase in size while maintaining their physical characteristics, yet adjusting shape to meet new functional requirements. The pudgy and relatively clumsy hands of a baby thus develop into incredibly versatile and highly articulate instruments in adults. Shells, by contrast, grow through sequential addition of similar modules. The first remains fixed as an inanimate object to which subsequent modules are attached — like rooms in an ever-growing structure — as the mollusk inside it expands its own body parts. The

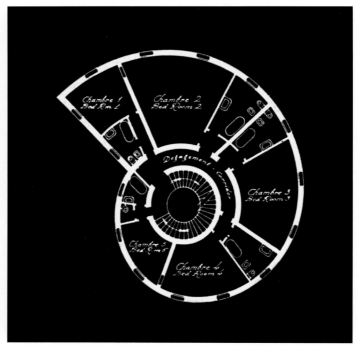

Two graphic reconstructions illustrating combined radial and rotational growth in organisms.

The first is a side view of *Haliotis assina*, where successive growth stages follow a Fibonacci sequence.

The second illustrates growth stages in *Archiectonica nobilis* — the pointed rectangles at right, whose base and height are determined by the width of the adjacent rotations, are all proportioned according to a golden spiral.

(From György Doczi's *The Power of Limits*, Shambala editions, Boston & London, 1981, pp. 54 and 55.)

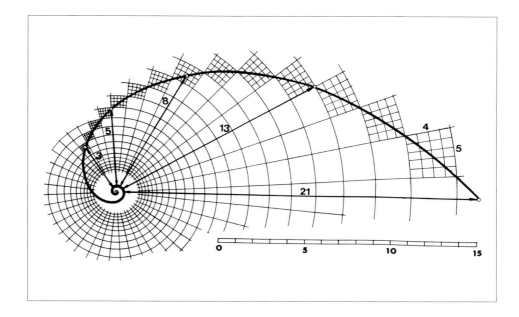

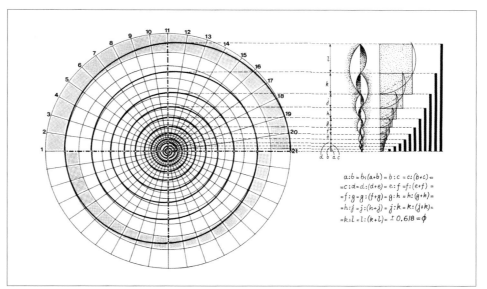

shell thus retains components that formed within it even after they are spent or their function is given over to newer parts; upon the death of the mollusk, the shell remains long after its inhabitant has decomposed. Like a real house, a shell outlives its builder and becomes a vessel for other occupants and for camouflage; or a place for a hermit crab to use as a protective mantle; or, ultimately, outside the marine environment as a collector's item.

Because of their size, portability and ease of handling, shells have not been reproduced artificially; instead they have been widely enjoyed and admired for their beauty. People have enjoyed touching their bright surfaces, holding them to their ears and listening to the sounds generated as air flows through them, or as happens with cowry shells (*Cypraea*), hearing a cycle of sounds reminiscent of crashing ocean waves.

Shells have inspired the realm of human imagination, influenced the Surrealist art world (including that of Marcel Duchamp) been buried in ancient tombs. Shells have served as geometric and abstract symbols among ancient civilizations, with spirals and stripes of converging lines having particularly deep significance. Shells were also put to practical use, for example as jewelry, and as receptacles to hold salt, ointments and perfumes.

The tower of the double helix staircase at the Châteaux de Chambord, France, c. 1519–47.

We also find shell symbols among animal figures in cathedrals or, due to their Christian connotations with the apostle James, as emblems along the pilgrimage to the tomb of Santiago de Compostella. Sandro Botticelli was the first painter to use the shell in other than a decorative manner by featuring a scallop shell (*Pecten* sp.) as a vessel in his *Birth of Venus* masterpiece. By using only half of this bivalve and removing any "animalistic" nature associated with it, the artist uses the shell as a harmonious backdrop for the human body as created by God, in his own image. After being placed in an exalted position, also echoed in a painting by Antonio da Correggio, the shell allegorically reappears as a cursed creature in Giovanni Bellini's work, where it is pictured as a human body wrapped in serpents. In Brueghel's visionary painting, mollusks are depicted as monsters.

At the same time, however, shells proved difficult to explain in philosophical terms and were seen as unusual items more like concrete inanimate objects than living things. Consequently they were placed among nature's marvels and part of the *Wunderkammer,* or cabinets of curiosities, in keeping with a time when travelers ventured afar to explore the world's oceans in search of exotic things to collect and study. Jacopo Zucchi's lavish painting, *Treasures of the Sea*, housed in the Borghese Gallery in Rome, is an open *Wunderkammer*, in which various types of shells and conchs are shown lying on grass or brandished like trophies by several people.

Amsterdam became the center of shell collections. It's not surprising, therefore. that one of Rembrandt's most beautiful engravings shows an image of *Conus*

marmoreus against a dark background. This black–and–white snail shell is covered by an exterior that sparkles intensely in the light, much like smooth cloth brought to life by an irregular surface pattern.

A portrayal by Thomas de Critz of one of the first great English collectors, John Tradescant, is housed in the Ashmolean Museum in Oxford. The picture shows him and his son next to a table packed with magnificent shells. In modern paintings, descriptive details are no longer emphasized, but shells have once again become symbols of the mysteries of the sea, as in the works of Odilon Redon, Marc Chagall and Paul Klee.

Shells have probably left their biggest mark in human endeavors in architecture. This is not simply the result of humans observing nature and exploring its visible forms and shapes, but also a reflection of the laws that are derived from them. This applies not only to the surfaces of shells and their growth processes, but also the simple designs these animals communicate to us.

The winding staircase, derived from the elliptical outline of the mollusk "house," has ancient origins. Although the Bible story of the Tower of Babel is told without specifying its shape, subsequent imaginary renditions by Brueghel or Athanasius Kircher are clearly refinements of the helical shell. In the description of the Temple of Solomon in the First Book of Kings, the three floors of the building are linked by a spiral staircase. In Palestine today we can still see a cylindrical ramp in Gideon's water cistern, carved into the rock prior to the 10th century B.C.

Félix Candela, restaurant,
Xochimilco, 1957–58.

Apollodorus of Damascus used a helical basis not only for the internal staircase in Trajan's Column but also to adorn the marble covering on which the emperor's accomplishments are carved; this was in accordance with the "continuous narrative method" that art historian Alois Riegl interpreted as typical of the neo-antique style. Countless other examples that make use of shell motifs can be found in Roman and medieval architecture, as well as in Islamic countries. Significant examples of the evolution of this architectural style include the two minarets of Samarra and the one of the Mosque of Ibn Tulun in Cairo; the vine of Saint Gilles built in 1142 for the abbey of the same name near Arles in Provence; the double-helix staircase in Châteaux de Chambord (likely inspired by Leonardo da Vinci); the Belvedere steps in the Vatican; and the legendary portal of the Palladio in the Carita convent in Venice.

Another formal motif that appears repeatedly in many bath basins in late antique architecture is the conch. We see it in the Temple of Artemis in Gerasa, in the catacombs of Kom el-Shogafa in Alexandria, and in Rome in the C mausoleum of the Vatican Necropolis. Donato Bramante picks it up again in the monumental stairway of the Abbey of Santa Maria del Popolo, making it a decorative emblem characteristic of the renaissance and baroque eras, a sculptural oddity that draws an analogy between the words "niche" and "cavity," the latter being synonymous with shell in both Italian and French.

In terms of symbolism, we also find a helical ramp at the top of the dome of the church of Sant'Ivo alla Sapienza, built by Francesco Borromini, who also kept a shell mounted on a brass pedestal in his cabinet of curiosities. This was seen as an essential component of the Borromini school of architecture in the 1600s; he explored a variety of novel concepts, none of which are considered definitive or beyond questioning. It is also interesting to point out that the architect did not rely on any particular species of shell in establishing a link between structure and decoration in the tower atop the church of Sant'Ivo. Although some decorative features of the tower were undoubtedly inspired by a pointed crown adorned with precious stones, elements like the repeating battlement and the vertical spacing between spirals bring

to mind similar harmonious elements in several species of the family Columbariidae, including *Columbarium pagodoides* or *Columbarium formosissimum*.

The shell motif played a very distinctive role in baroque sculpture and architecture because of its organic plasticity and its association with the aquatic environment. We see it therefore as a central character of fountains, like those of Bernini's Triton Fountain and the Fontana delle Api (Fountain of Bees). Shells, along with rocks, are also dominant themes in Rococo plasterwork, which combined torsion and shell undulation into a unique decorative form in which each object appears alternately split, fluid and foamlike before seemingly melting into forms lacking structure and rigidity. Although this style of sculpture does not show any specific types of shells, it does draw on oysters to represent undulation layers that are intertwined with each other. This creates the spatial impression of undulating motion similar to the cyclical movement of the sea.

We can appreciate, therefore, that the shape of shells has inspired architecture since its very beginnings. However, only during the last century, with the arrival of Organic Architecture and Expressionism, did this reach a pinnacle, whereby not only were the spatial and decorative aspects of shells utilized to the fullest, but also the organisms themselves and their basic structure. The spiral as ramp-covering is

Mautizio Sacripanti, "Idea of a space in motion," proposal for the Italian pavilion at Expo Osaka, 1970 (from Maurizio Sacripanti's *City of the Frontier*, Bulzoni, Rome, 1973).

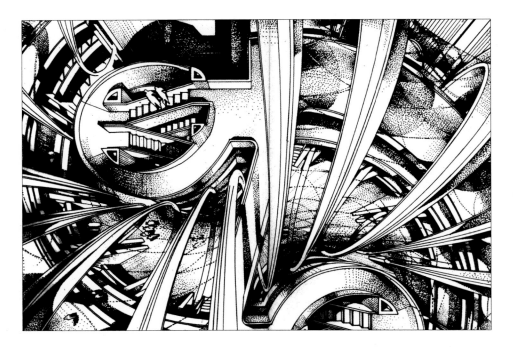

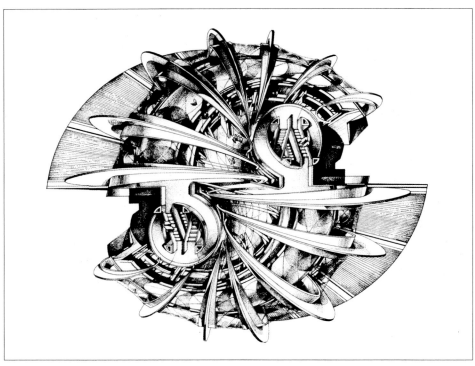

evident in the work of Frank Lloyd Wright in his 1924 design of the Sugarloaf Mountain Planetarium in Maryland and, much later, in the monument to Harum al-Rashid in Baghdad in 1957. Although both these projects unfortunately only reached the design phase rather than becoming some of the finest monuments of our times, the rising helix can be seen in New York's Guggenheim Museum (1959). It is reminiscent of the theme of Borromini's Sant'Ivo church, or of what was created by the engineer Giuseppe Momo in his splendid dual ascending staircases in the Vatican Museums.

With the advent of Art Nouveau during the early 1900s, the shell motif had moved beyond the purely decorative through expanding space with winding helical staircases, something new technology now made possible through strength and support. For example, the transparent ceilings in the celebrated Paris Metro stations created by Hector Guimard bring to mind the radial motif of scallop shells. In the ,model proposed by Vladimir Tatlin for the *Monument to the Third International*, a gastropod shell becomes a winding strip from which lines of force extend, bracing three geometric solids that support the convention hall. This image projected great symbolic value, as taught during the October Revolution, but Soviet authorities suppressed it immediately without regret. In the *Alpine Architecture* of Bruno Taut (1919), a helical tower located in the middle of a lake provides access to a flight of stairs leading to the Crystal House, a utopian image of a new society free of wars. Following World War II, after the construction of the Guggenheim and Bruce Goff's Bavinger House, Jørn Utzon revived the shell theme in a very innovative fashion. He did not rely on any specific type of shell, but used shell shapes to develop a varied, repeat pattern as unique modules based on gastropod coverings. The curved shells of the opera house that has become the defining landmark of the Sydney skyline have successfully explored the symbolism of repetition, both acoustical and musical, through concrete waves reflective of the marine life of the surrounding landscape. A similar visionary potential is evident in Maurizio Sacripanti's *Italian Pavilion for the World Expo in Osaka*, which unfortunately only exists on paper. The building, which was supposed to move and pulsate like a living organism, paraphrased in broad terms the structure of *Epitonium scalare*, a conch much sought after by collectors and once so rare that near-perfect imitations were manufactured in China. These shells feature two large circular tubes, wound into seven interlinked rings to form a scaled cylinder that seems to whorl and twist to a pointed top. Like an Escher drawing, the shell's spacing has an ambiguous quality, with a rhythmic, pulsating aspect that extends into the fourth dimension of time as the conch grows. The spirals designed in 1979 by Philip Johnson for the Chapel of Thanksgiving in Dallas are far less fanciful and convincing as are those of César Pelli in his helical towers of 1980.

In assessing what direction architectural efforts will take during the first years of the new century, one can say that "learning from shells" might be one way to recapture the bewildered "naturalness" of the constructive form.

A World of Curiosities

To admire a shell is to unconsciously pay homage to the mollusk that created it. These animals, the epitome of softness and slowness, are in reality formidable builders, capable of an architectural prowess probably unsurpassed in the animal kingdom. With about 120,000 species, each acutely distinct from each other, these creatures have not yet ceased to astonish us as they reveal their myriad wonders. It is enough to satisfy the curiosity of a collector for an entire lifetime. Proof of this lies in the exceptional collection of Jacques and Rita Senders, which was started 50 years ago and continues to grow, fueled by the same enthusiasm as that of their very first day of collecting. The photographs in this book (which displays only a sampling of that collection) give the reader a glimpse of the extraordinary diversity of these animals.

Mollusk Anatomy

All mollusks share a common characteristic — a soft body. They also have a head, a muscular foot and a visceral mass that contains their organs. The visceral mass is covered by a fold of skin: the mantle. Overflowing from the visceral mass, the mantle forms a pocket: the palleal cavity. It is within this chamber that exchanges with the environment occur. Here is the location of the respiratory system (gills or lungs, according to the animal's lifestyle), as well as the openings of the digestive, excretory and reproductive organs.

From Head to Foot

The mollusk's head contains the mouth, as well as receptors sensitive to light, touch, spatial orientation, movement and chemical stimuli — but not to sound as we perceive it. The foot is muscular and contains many gaps that are capable of filling with blood. As its name implies, its main use is for locomotion. One unusual characteristic of mollusks is that their blood contains hemocyanin, a copper-containing protein used as a means to carry oxygen in the bloodstream — similar to the iron-rich hemoglobin in human blood. However, unlike human blood, which turns red when oxygenated, the chemically based pigments in hemocyanin cause a mollusk's oxygenated blood to become blue.

The Magical Mantle

The mantle is undoubtedly the most mysterious and fascinating component of these animals since it is directly involved in secreting the shell. This workload is shared by two activity zones: the border of the mantle is assigned the task of enlarging the shell, whereas the rest of the mantle's surface is dedicated to the thickening of the shell. The mantle's border is also charged with making a hard substance, named conchiolin (it is chemically similar to chitin, which forms the exoskeletons of insects and crustaceans). This substance forms a thin external film on the shell — the periostracum — a kind of protective varnish. Underneath, we find a thick calcareous layer whose crystals, in the form of prisms, are more or less

Pleurotomariidae
Perotrochus midas
Distribution: Bahamas, in deep water
Average Size: 3.1 inches (8 cm)
Frequency: Rare

Strombidae
Strombus canarium
Distribution: Southwestern Pacific,
in shallow water
Average size: 2.4 inches (6 cm)
Frequency: Common

perpendicular to the shell's surface. Growing within this conchiolin matrix, these crystals enlarge the holes until a thin film remains between each one of them. In fact, this second layer, the ostracum, contains very little of the conchiolin and is made up of a very resistant composite material.

A final zone comes in direct contact with the mantle and is fabricated by its entire surface: it is the hypostracum. Here, the crystals are deposited in lamellae, parallel to the surface. Depending on the species, the crystals are composed of either calcite or aragonite. It is only when the crystals are composed of aragonite that they have the ability to produce the splendid iridescence found on the inside of shells known as nacre, or mother-of-pearl. Unfortunately, there are far fewer aragonite-producing mollusks than calcite-producers, and therefore fewer shells with nacre than without.

Unique Specimens

The building activity of the mantle is not uniform either in time or in modality. When the building activity ceases during a particular period, the result is a striation. If, at any given moment, the activity becomes intensified, the shell obtains a hill. At a particular site, the folding of the edge coupled with a strong thickening function may produce a bump, even a spike.

On the other hand, pigment-secreting cells are also at work. During growth, whether they function all at the same time, or in groups, over long or short periods, they will give birth to a band, a trait or a distinguishing mark.

Predator and Prey

In building its shell, the mollusk must gather a large quantity of calcium. This material is gathered directly from the water or gained from its diet. Aside from bivalves, which are content to just filter food from the water, many mollusks have the ability to graze or scrape their food from various surfaces. To accomplish this,

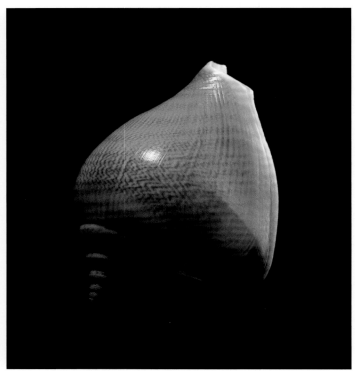

Glossidae

Glossus humanus

Distribution: From Norway to the
Mediterranean, from 32– 9,840 feet
(10–3,000 m)
Average size: 3.1 inches (8 cm)
Frequency: Locally abundant

they use an organ with a very unique and constantly changing morphology according to their way of life: the radula. This is a chitinous blade equipped with several rows of teeth, resting within a muscular mass known as the odontophore. These muscles permit a variety of movements, analogous to those of a tongue — making the radula a sort of very raspy tongue.

In grazing mollusks, the teeth are numerous and identical. The animal uses its odontophore to lash out at bits of the surface it is moving along. If it scrapes off a large morsel, the radula will then need to further shred this fragment into the mouth.

Vegetarian shell animals have bladelike teeth they use to split the cell walls of algae and then suck out their contents. The teeth, consisting solely of chitin, are quickly worn down and replaced regularly by new ones. The radula functions like a rolling carpet, progressing from the back to the front.

In carnivorous species, the radula is smaller and has fewer teeth, but they are longer and pointier. Sometimes sharp and crooked, they enable the animal to capture its prey and bring it to its mouth. Certain predators manage to penetrate the shells of other mollusks by wearing them down through rotating movements of their radula. Others, by using the foot as a suction cup and the edge of their shell as a leveraging tool, manage to pry the two halves of a bivalve (for example, an oyster) apart in order to feed on it. By rubbing its shell against the joint of the two valves of a mollusk, some carnivorous species open a breach by which they can devour their prey. Some will even set themselves up on the surface of an oyster while waiting patiently for it to open, then shove the edge of their shell into the gap and feed upon the oyster. The most enterprising of them have just a few teeth (sometimes only one), which are very long and equipped with a venom canal that releases a neurotoxin. Thus equipped, they become true hunters of worms, mollusks or even fish.

Nassariidae

Bullia sendersi

Distribution: Kenya

Average size: 1.6 inches (4 cm)

Frequency: Locally abundant

Comments: Found in wet sand during low tide

Clavagellidae

Brechites penis

Distribution: Indian Ocean and the Antilles, buried in sand several yards deep

Average size: 4 inches (10 cm)

Frequency: Common

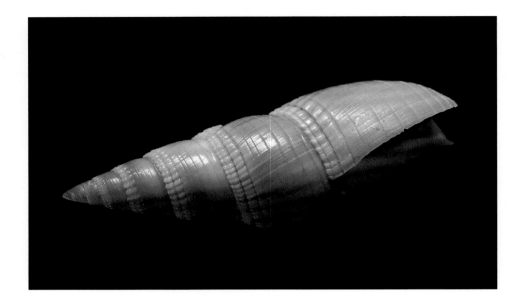

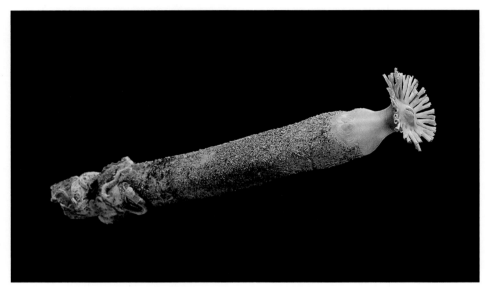

Whatever their own diets, mollusks are important in the diets of other animals, and they are equipped with defense mechanisms to protect themselves. The first and simplest response of a mollusk is to retract into its shell. To avoid being swallowed whole or having its carapace broken, some have shells with spines or very sharp spikes.

Camouflage is another defense mechanism, and the shell may display the same coloration as the substrate in the mollusk's habitat in order to blend with it. Some mollusks even incorporate external elements (bits of coral, shells or stones) during their growth phase to take the camouflage defense even further.

Upon the approach of a predator such as a starfish, scallops can open and close their valves quickly to empty water, enabling them to swim away. Other mollusks move by "walking": folding their foot under themselves, then abruptly unfolding it. Still others are able to swim from one rock to the next through undulating motions from their mantle border. However, these travels, whenever made, mostly serve for either flight or feeding — although they also allow the sexes to move closer together.

Sex and Gender

In the presence of a female ready to lay eggs, a sedentary male mollusk will emit a cloud of sperm into the water. The female in contact with this cloud will then

Cardiidae
Cardita megastropha
Distribution: Tropical Pacific, in the sand
in moderately deep water
Average size: 1.6 inches (4 cm)
Frequency: Locally common

Cardiidae
Frangum unedo
Distribution: Western Pacific
Average size: 1.6 inches (4 cm)
Frequency: Common and abundant

Turbinellidae
Columbarium harrisae
Distribution: Australia
Average size: 2.8 inches (7 cm)
Frequency: Relatively common
Observations: Often found in fishing
nets but rarely in good condition

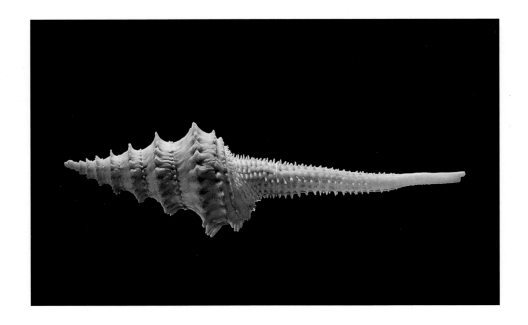

release her eggs and fertilization will occur in the waters surrounding the two partners. This method is not without risk to the fertilized eggs thus formed, nor to the larvae they will develop into. The chances that a fertilized egg will make it to adulthood are about 1 in 100,000. As a result, in this reproductive method it becomes necessary to produce a huge amount of eggs (at times several million) to ensure sufficient reproduction. The odds are improved when sperm are aspired into the female's palleal cavity. The eggs are then produced and fertilized on site and are incubated safely within the animal itself instead of being released in the environment.

Mobile species have the advantage of being able to undergo internal fertilization thanks to a copulatory organ that short-circuits the aquatic phase. The female is then able to greatly reduce the number of eggs produced, thus saving her energy and providing substantial protection for the eggs. With this advantage, these fertilized eggs sometimes spend their incubation in the female's interior; although, in the majority of species, the eggs are deposited in a suitable location. There, depending on the species, the development occurs to the first and second larval stages, or even to a later stage. Some species no longer emerge at the larval stage; most of their development occurs within the egg, from which emerges a fully formed, tiny mollusk.

Are the resulting mollusks male or female? Actually, depending on the species, a given individual may not live through its life as only one gender — as either a male or a female. It can remain male during its youth, then become female thereafter. In other species, it undergoes changes in gender several times, back and forth during its lifetime. A large number of species have resolved the problem simply by being hermaphrodites. Parthenogenetic reproduction (self-fertilization) even occurs in some mollusk species.

The Human-Mollusk Relationship

They grow, they multiply and they are found in a large number of diverse forms everywhere on our planet. Mollusks could obviously not escape the notice of human beings.

Turbinidae

Angaria tyria

Distribution: Indo-Pacific and
eastern Australia
Average size: 1.6 inches (4 cm)
Frequency: Quite rare

Turbinidae

Angaria poppei

Distribution: The Philippines
Average size: 2 inches (5 cm),
including spines
Frequency: Uncommon

From prehistoric times, mollusks have constituted a food source for humans, as seen in the evidence of enormous piles of empty shells at archaeological sites. Since those early days of humankind, mollusks have continued to play this role of foodstuff, with more or less success depending on the time period and location.

For sailors landing on an island following a long period at sea, the presence of shells represented a veritable manna after the malnutrition and privations they endured. Throughout time, coastal populations have consumed this precious source of protein, which was relatively simple to harvest — a job that was usually reserved for women and children to perform.

However, once the meat was consumed, the mollusk did not lose all its appeal. The shells have proven to be useful, not just for the food source they provided. This is an attribute all the more precious since they are sometimes found in areas poor in natural resources (such as an atoll, for example) or without strong industry.

Fishers used shells as baling tools and their nacre to form spoon bait on their fishing hooks. Some shells were deep enough to use them to create a makeshift adze when (or where) metal was not available. Some shells served as coconut rasps, others as knives to peel fruit or vegetables, while others still as axe-, lance- and arrow-sharpening tools. Pearl oysters became musical instruments when fashioned into castanets. Larger shells were appropriately pierced and used to trumpet calls for reunions or religious ceremonies.

However, the dietary and practical functions of shells are not the only ones humans have exploited. Their astonishing shapes, rare and suggestive, and their delicate colorations predestined them for further use.

They have long served (and continue to do so) as decorative elements; the shell has been used whole or in parts in jewelry, masks, clothing, totems and housing. Jewelry has been encrusted with nacre, as have a variety of commonplace and

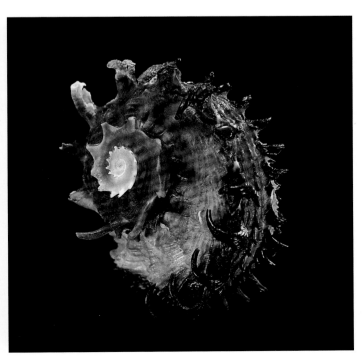

Conidae
Conus gloriamaris
Distribution: The Philippines and
Solomon Islands
Average size: 3.5 inches (9 cm)
Frequency: Somewhat rare
Observations: For a long time, only
one specimen of this species was
known to exist, and as a result it
was the most treasured species
for more than two centuries.

Strombidae
Strombus labiatus
Distribution: Western Pacific, in
shallow water
Average size: 2 inches (5 cm)
Frequency: Relatively common

religious items (including caskets, mirrors, crosses and sacred relics). Up until about 1950, they were used to make sewing buttons. However, it is in the form of pearls that the nacre has been the most highly esteemed. In antiquity, pearls were much valued by the Greeks; the Romans also treasured them. This fascination has endured right up until today. Apart from its obvious beauty, the fact that more than 10,000 pearl oysters must be collected in order to discover just one natural, marketable pearl, certainly adds to the emotional charge of observing a fine specimen. The introduction of pearl oyster cultivation has undoubtedly saved the lives of many pearl divers and, to a certain extent, the very existence of the species. It may have also changed our attitude toward these beautiful gemstones.

Apart from their decorative role, it is also clear that, in many cases, the presence of ornamental shells carries a symbolic meaning. Shells can reveal themselves to be vital, utilitarian and practical. However, a significant reason for why humankind is so interested in them is the simple existence of the shells themselves.

Collections and Conservation

Already in evidence during the Roman era, for a long time, shell collecting was a pursuit limited to people of royalty or nobility. The collection of the renowned naturalist Jean-Baptiste de Monet, Chevalier de Lamarck, contributed to theories of evolution. With the advent of exploratory and scientific voyages along with societal changes, collections multiplied. This became no longer a privilege reserved solely for nobility but extended to the well-to-do, some of whom

Strombidae
Strombus pipus
Distribution: Indo-Pacific
Average size: 2 inches (5 cm)
Frequency: Uncommon
Observation: Relatively rare with
a dark interior

Epitoniidae
Epitonium pallasi
Distribution: Indo-Pacific
Average size: 1.6 inches (4 cm)
Frequency: Somewhat common

devoted their entire fortunes to the pursuit. Today it is no longer necessary to dedicate a fortune to have a very interesting shell collection, but other challenges are faced by the amateur. The conchologist must adopt responsible behavior in order to offset the dangers of pursuing his or her passion.

As with other organisms living on the planet, mollusks are subject to organic, chemical and nuclear pollutants. Several species are endangered or at the point of becoming extinct. Even if collectors are not the major threat to these animals, each one of us must reduce our environmental impact as much as possible. While the gathering of empty seashells on the seashores does not pose a threat, where living mollusks are concerned we must respect certain rules and guidelines. The following are three recommendations by the great conchologist whose shells are displayed in this book:

- Limit the number of shells gathered. Ideally, select a single, exemplary representative so as not to collect extras that will be redundant in a collection and thus will have died for nothing.

- Always have the necessary materials available for good conservation of the collected specimens.

- Avoid, to the highest possible degree, any modifications to the environment in which you are collecting the shells; for example, return a stone to its initial position after having turned it over.

Behavior that respects nature does not need to reduce a conchologist's passion for collecting shells. In the rare cases where collectors might deprive themselves of a capture, they will hopefully have the satisfaction of realizing that by making the decision, future generations of their children and grandchildren may well have the ability to become happy conchologists themselves.

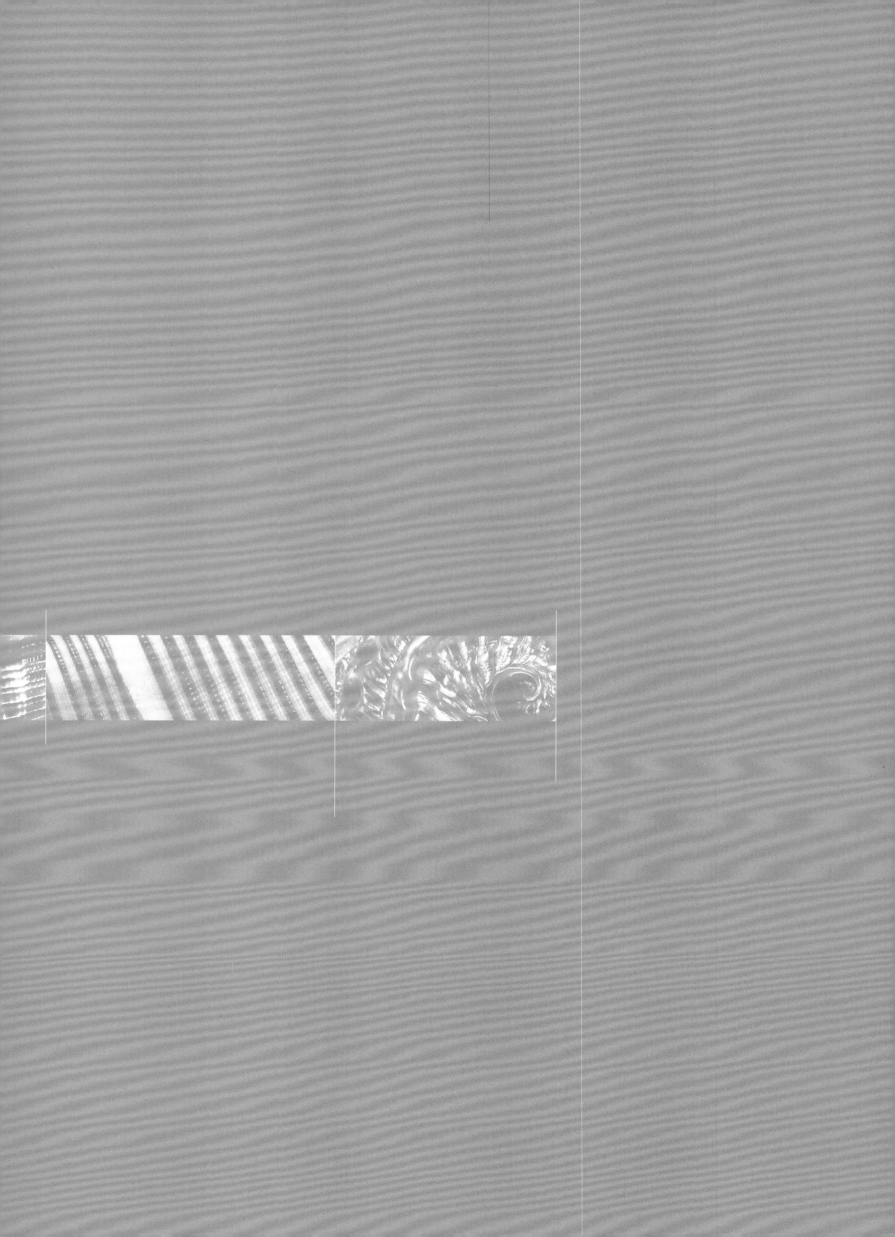

The Art of Shells

When artists realize that their imagination is limited,
that everything they can think of in terms of form and
color, nature has already done better and always offers
something newer and richer, then our poor
imagination even at its richest seems rather
monotonous ...

Pierre-Auguste Renoir
Grammaire, 1883–1884

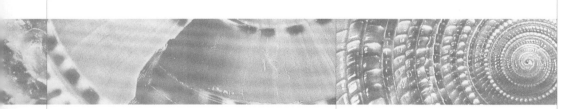

Aporrhaididae
Aporrhais seresianus
Distribution: Atlantic Ocean from Norway
to the Mediterranean, in deep waters
Average size: 1.2 inches (3 cm)
Frequency: Uncommon

Aporrhaididae
Aporrhais pespelicanis ▸▸
Distribution: Atlantic Ocean from the
Lofoten Islands to the Mediterranean, to a
depth of 460 feet (140 m)
Average size: 1.6 inches (4 cm)
Frequency: Common

*Captions go with pictures from left to right
unless otherwise indicated.

Architectonicidae
Architectonica maxima
Distribution: Western Pacific Ocean
Average size: 2.2 inches (5.5 cm)
Frequency: Fairly common
Observations: Named because it is given to architecture students as a model

▶

Architectonicidae
Architectonica nobilis
Distribution: Western Atlantic Ocean from
the United States to Brazil; Pacific Ocean
from Mexico to Peru
Average size: 1.6 inches (4 cm)
Frequency: Locally common

Architectonicidae
Philippia radiata
Distribution: Western Pacific Ocean and
Mozambique
Average size: 0.6 inches (1.5 cm)
Frequency: Common
Observations: Sometimes thrown on the
beach by wave activity

▼

Architectonicidae
Architectonica perspectiva
Distribution: Indo-Pacific, in shallower
waters, on and in sand
Average size: 1.6 inches (4 cm)
Frequency: Common, occasionally abundant

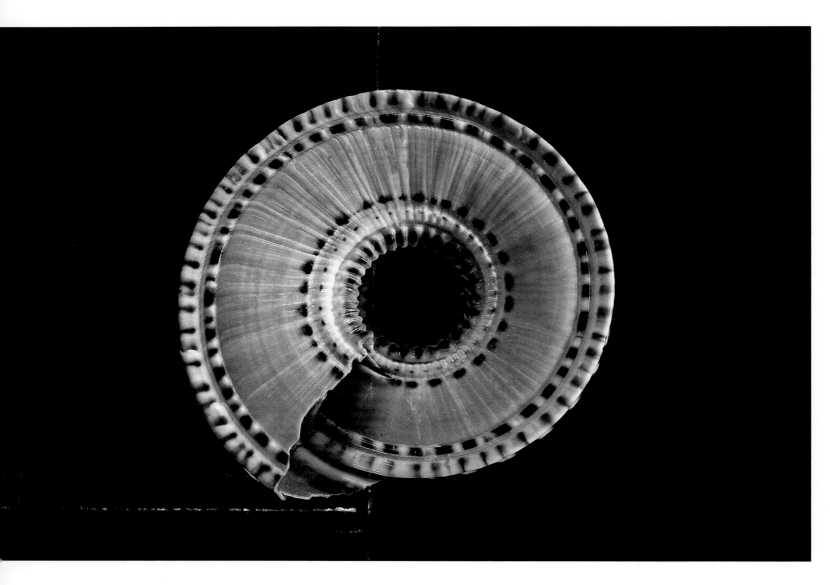

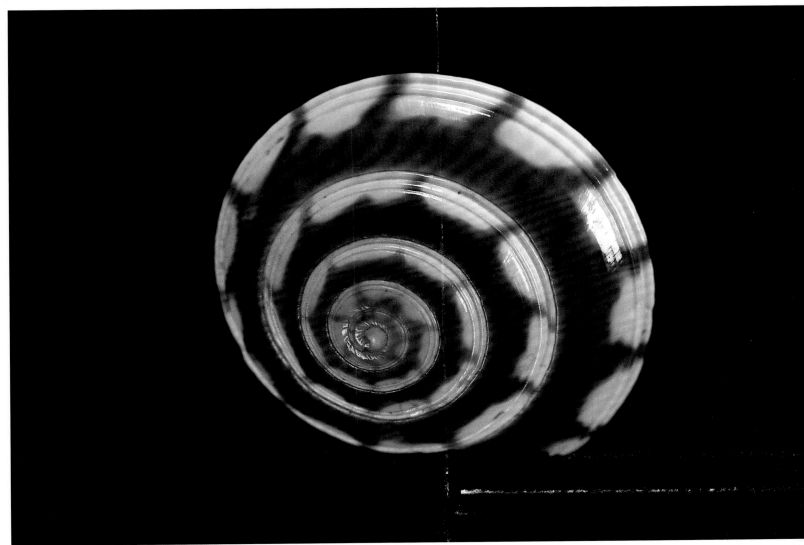

Buccinidae
Babylonia areolata
Distribution: Southeast Asia, on sand at
32–65 feet (10–20 m)
Average size: 2.4 inches (6 cm)
Frequency: Common
Observations: Common in Asian markets
as with other *Babylonia*

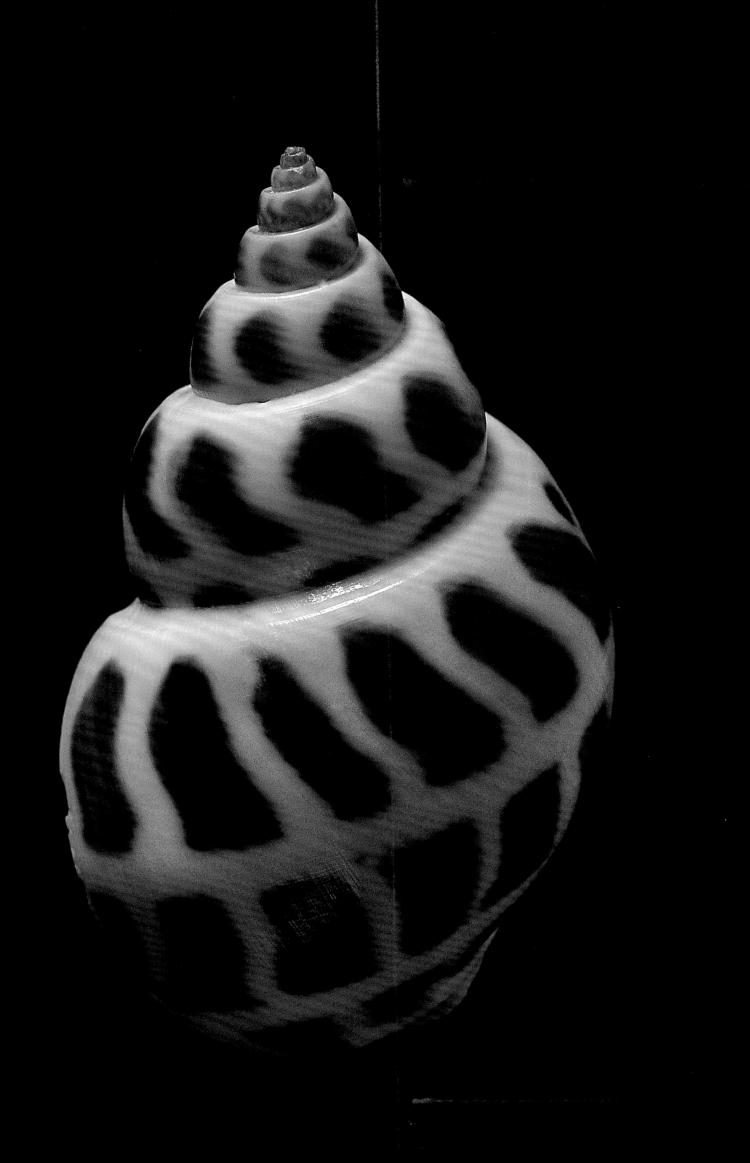

Buccinidae
Babylonia papillaris
Distribution: South Africa, to depths of
325 feet (100 m)
Average size: 1.4 inches (3.5 cm)
Frequency: Uncommon

Buccinidae
Babylonia papillaris
Distribution: South Africa, to depths of
325 feet (100 m)
Average size: 1.4 inches (3.5 cm)
Frequency: Uncommon

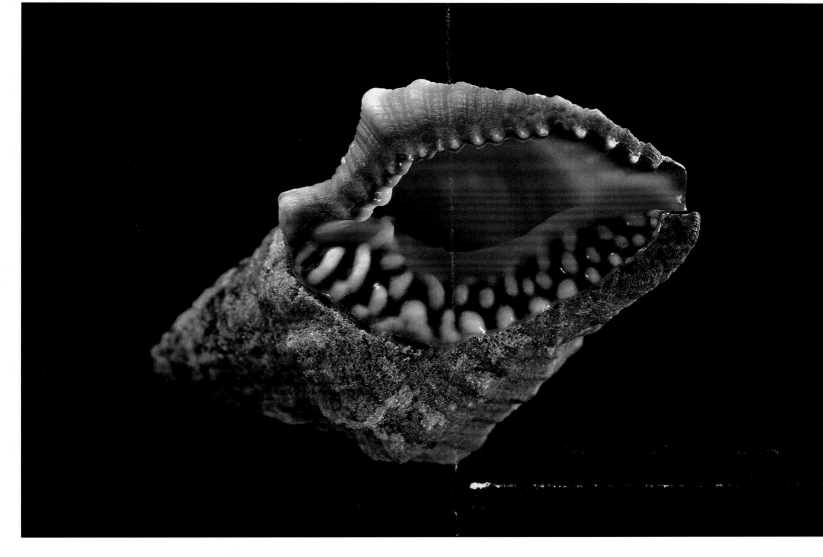

Buccinidae
Neptunea contraria
Distribution: Western Atlantic Ocean,
widely distributed in deep water
Average size: 3.1 inches (8 cm)
Frequency: Rarely common
Observations: This species is naturally
left-whorled.

▼
Buccinidae
Buccinum politum
Distribution: Indo-Pacific and Taiwan
Average size: 2 inches (5 cm)
Frequency: Common

▶

Buccinidae
Phos senticosus
Distribution: Western Pacific Ocean
Average size: 1.4 inches (3.5 cm)
Frequency: Common

▼

Buccinidae
Cantharus undosus
Distribution: Tropical Indo-Pacific, on rocks
and dead coral
Average size: 1.2 inches (3 cm)
Frequency: Common
Observations: Not to be confused with
Cantharidus (Trochidae)

Buccinidae
Phos senticosus
Distribution: Western Pacific Ocean
Average size: 1.4 inches (3.5 cm)
Frequency: Common

Buccinidae
Engina alveolata
Distribution: Indo-Pacific in shallow waters
Average size: 0.8 inch (2 cm)
Frequency: Common

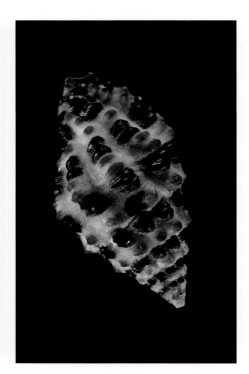

Bullidae
Bulla striata
Distribution: Atlantic Ocean, from Florida
to Mexico and the Mediterranean;
intertidal zones
Average size: 0.8 inch (2 cm)
Frequency: Locally abundant

Campanilidae
Campanile symbolicum
Distribution: Western Australia, widely
distributed to depths of 32 feet (10 m)
Average size: 7.1 inches (18 cm)
Frequency: Locally uncommon

Cancellariidae
Trigonostoma pellucida
Distribution: The Philippines
Average size: 1 inch (2.5 cm)
Frequency: Uncommon
Observations: Some *Trigonostoma* possess a spiral with independent turnings, not unlike a corkscrew.

Cassidae
Cypraecassis rufa
Distribution: Indo-Pacific
Average size: 5.1 inches (13 cm)
Frequency: Common to almost uncommon
due to frequent harvesting
Observations: Used since antiquity in Italy
to fabricate cameo jewelry

▶

Cassidae

Cassis norai

Distribution: Island of Cape Verde

Average size: 2 inches (5 cm)

Frequency: Rare

Observations: First described in 1995

▼

Cassidae

Cypraecassis tenuis

Distribution: Southern California to the
Equator and the Galapagos Islands

Average size: 3.1 inches (8 cm)

Frequency: Uncommon

Observations: Occasionally thrown on the
beach by wave activity

Cassidae

Cypraecassis testiculus

Distribution: Southeastern Florida to Brazil,
in shallow water

Average size: 2 inches (5 cm)

Frequency: Common

Cassidae

Cassis vibex

Distribution: Indo-Pacific

Average size: 2 inches (5 cm)

Frequency: Fairly common

Observations: Common via dredging

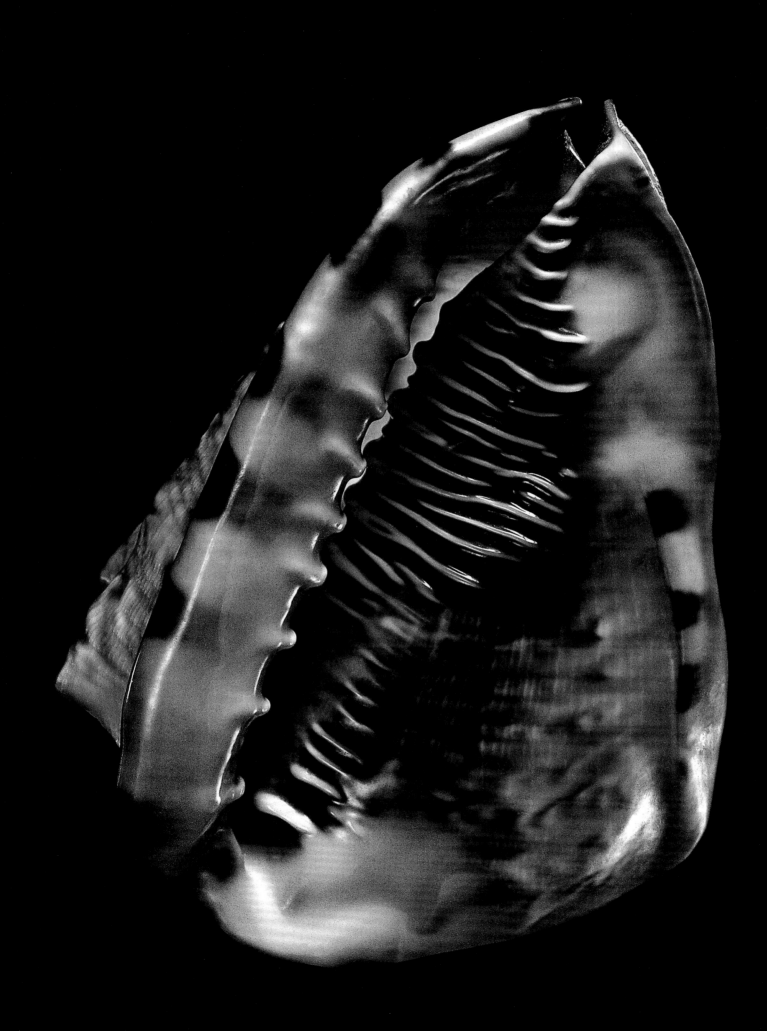

Cassidae

Phalium umbilicatum

Distribution: Hawaii, widely distributed
down to deep water

Average size: 2 inches (5 cm)

Frequency: Rare

▶

Cassidae

Galeodea echinophora

Distribution: The Mediterranean, widely distributed, down to deep water

Average size: 2 inches (5 cm)

Frequency: Uncommon

Cassidae

Phalium craticulatum

Distribution: East Africa, Mozambique to South Africa, in deep water

Average size: 2 inches (5 cm)

Frequency: Uncommon

▼

Cassidae

Semicassis semigranosom

Distribution: Southern Australia and Tasmania, on sand, widely distributed down to very deep water

Average size: 1.6 inches (4 cm)

Frequency: Common

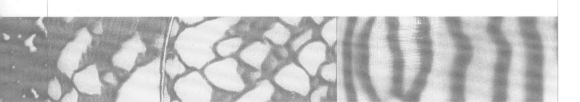

Conidae
Conus bengalensis
Distribution: Bay of Bengal, to depths of
65 feet (20 m)
Average size: 3.1 inches (8 cm)
Frequency: Moderately rare

▶

Conidae

Conus milneedwardsi clytospira

Distribution: India and Mozambique

Average size: 4.7 inches (12 cm)

Frequency: Rare

Observations: This is the rarest of all *Conus milneedwardsi*

▼

Conidae

Conus excelsus

Distribution: The Philippines

Average size: 2.8 inches (7 cm)

Frequency: Rare

Observations: Its high spire makes this a very elegant cone.

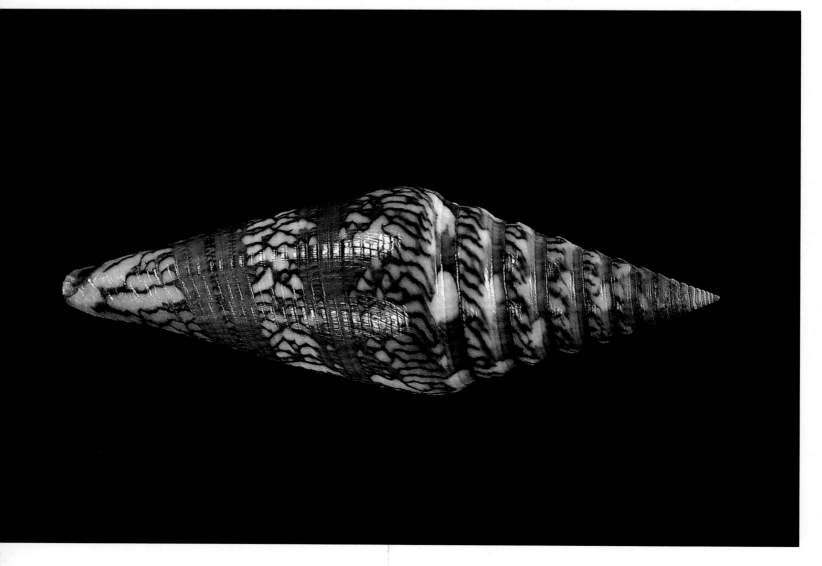

Conidae

Conus milneedwardsi clytospira

Distribution: India and Mozambique

Average size: 4.7 inches (12 cm)

Frequency: Rare

Observations: This is the rarest of all *Conus milneedwardsi*

►
Conidae
Conus cedonulli caledonicus
Distribution: Barbados
Average size: 2 inches (5 cm)
Frequency: Very rare

▼
Conidae
Conus eburneus
Distribution: The Philippines
Average size: 4.5 cm
Frequency: Common
Observations: Large variety of shapes and
colors

Conidae
Conus eburneus polyglotta
Distribution: The Philippines
Average size: 1.8 inches (4.5 cm)
Frequency: Common
Observations: The most coveted of the
Conus eburneus

Conidae
Conus vidua
Distribution: Madagascar, the Philippines
and Japan
Average size: 2 inches (5 cm)
Frequency: Fairly common
Observations: Once named *Conus bandanus
f. vidua*

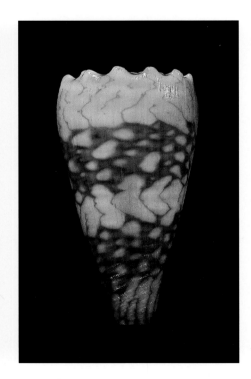

▶

Conidae

Conus behelokensis

(*Pennaceus behelokensis*)

Distribution: South of Madagascar

Average size: 2 inches (5 cm)

Frequency: Rare

Observations: Discovered and named in 1989

Conidae

Conus sanguinolentus

Distribution: Very widespread: all of the Indo-Pacific, in shallow waters

Average size: 1.2 inches (3 cm)

Frequency: Common

▼

Conidae

Conus zebroides

Distribution: Angola

Average size: 1.2 inches (3 cm)

Frequency: Uncommon

Observations: Synonymous with *Conus bulbus*

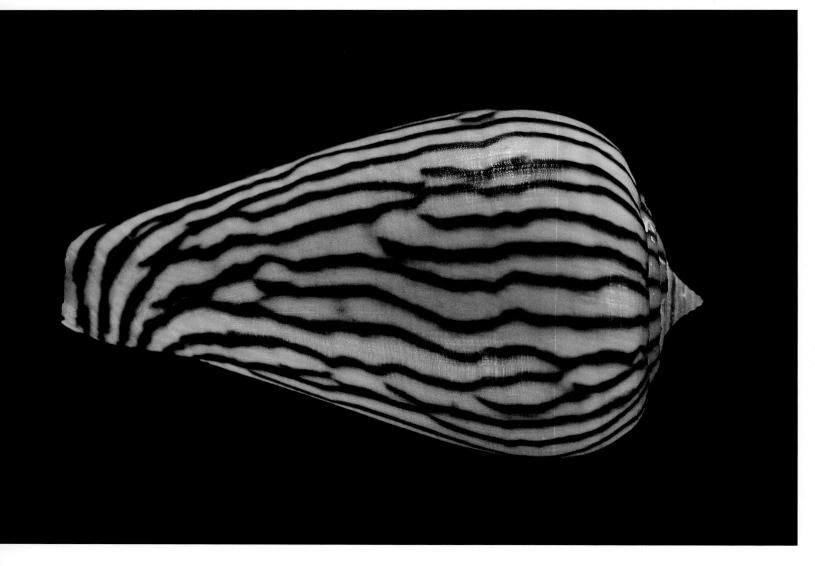

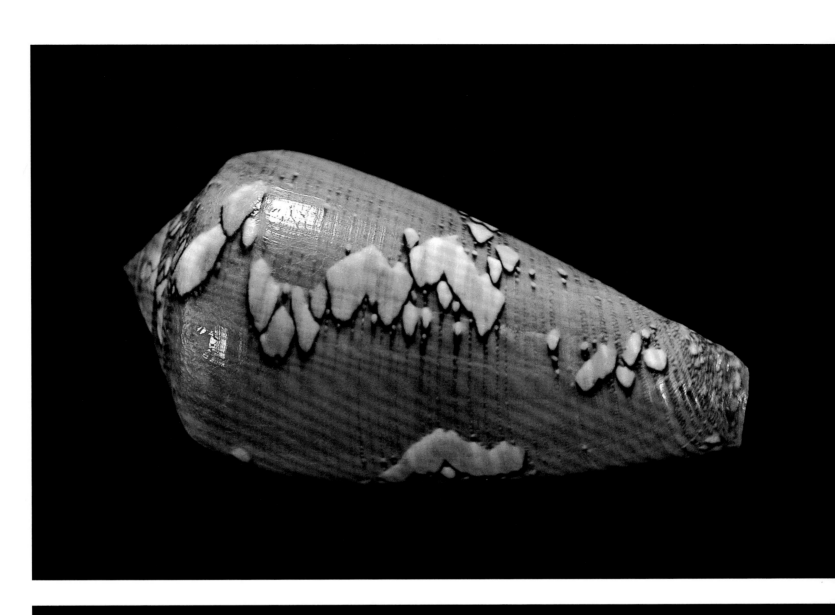

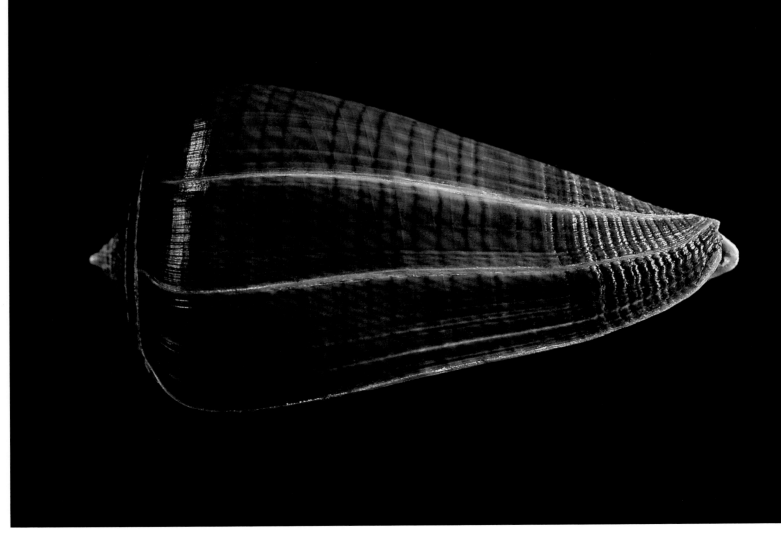

Coralliophilidae
Mipus vicdani
Distribution: The Philippines, in deep water
Average size: 1.8 inches (4.5 cm)
Frequency: Fairly rare

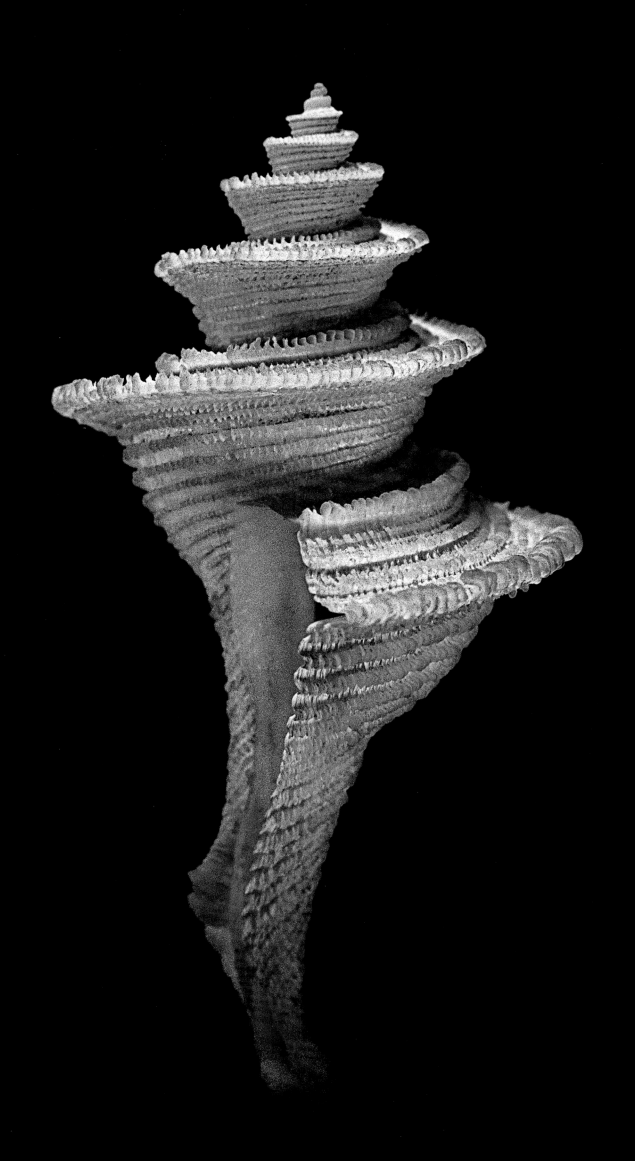

►

Coralliophilidae
Latiaxis sp.
Distribution: Indo-Pacific
Average size: 1.6 inches (4 cm)

▼

Coralliophilidae
Latiaxis mawae
Distribution: Japan
Average size: 1.8 inches (4.5 cm)
Frequency: Locally common
Observations: As with most of the
Coralliophilidae, it is not easy to find
a perfect example.

Coralliophilidae
Latiaxis sp.
Distribution: Indo-Pacific
Average size: 1.6 inches (4 cm)

Cypraeidae

Cypraea leucodon

Distribution: The Philippines and the
Maldives

Average size: 2.8 inches (7 cm)

Frequency: Rare

Observations: Long of unknown origin, until
recently this species has been one of the
most desired by collectors; however, for
several years Filipinos have harvested a
certain quantity thanks to tangle nets left
for several nights in deep water.

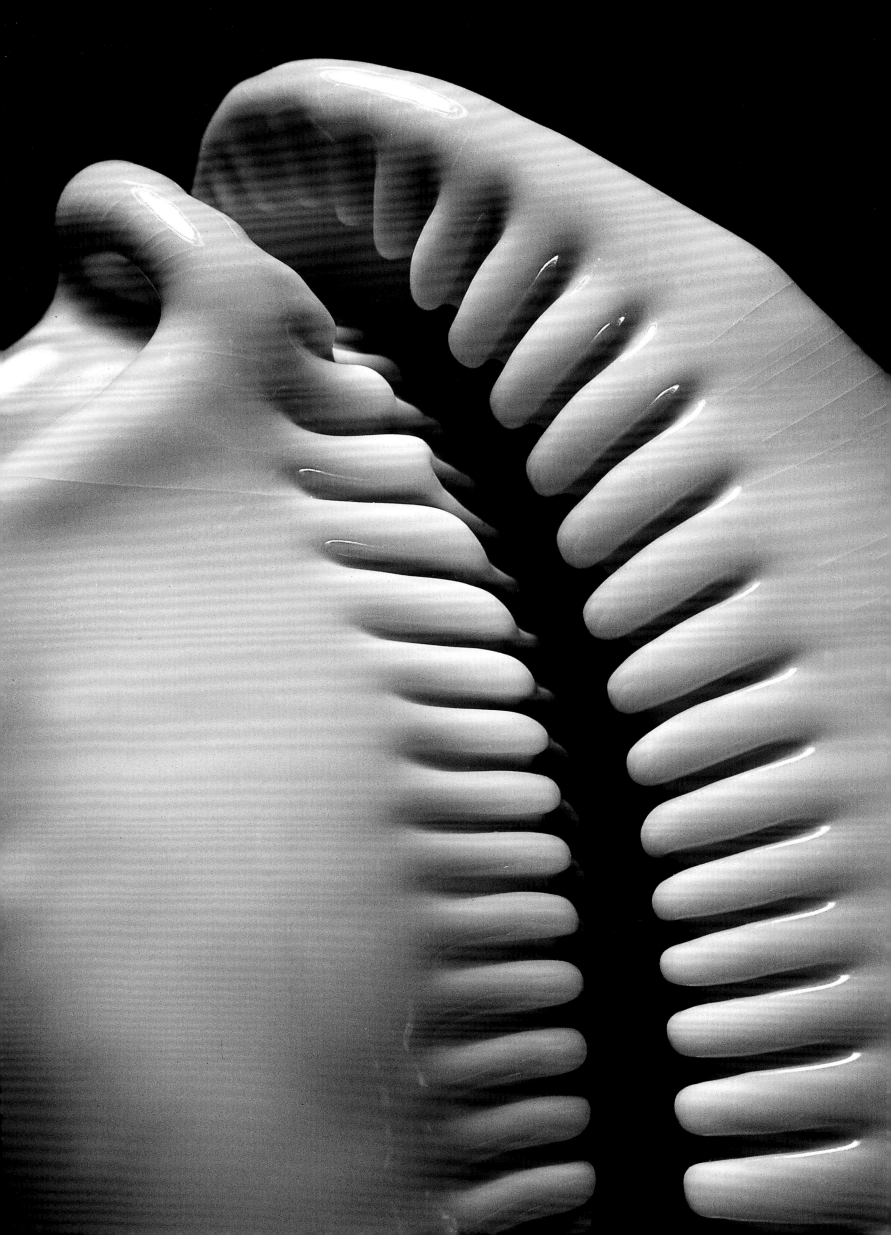

▶

Cypraeidae
Cypraea aurantium
Distribution: The Philippines to Polynesia
Average size: 3.1 inches (8 cm)
Frequency: Moderately rare
Observations: Emblem of the ancient Fijian
chieftains

▼

Cypraeidae
Cypraea marginata
Distribution: Western and southern
Australia; lives on sponges (which it feeds
on) to a depth of 820 feet (250 m)
Average size: 2 inches (5 cm)
Frequency: Rare

Cypraeidae
Cypraea guttata
Distribution: Southwest Pacific and Japan,
on coral reefs and to average depths
Average size: 2.8 inches (7 cm)
Frequency: Rare

Cypraeidae
Cypraea arabica
Distribution: All of Indo-Pacific region,
on coral reefs in deep water
Average size: 2.4 inches (6 cm)
Frequency: Very common

▶

Cypraeidae
Cypraea mappa
Distribution: The Indo-Pacific on coral reefs
Average size: 2.4 inches (6 cm)
Frequency: Uncommon

Cypraeidae
Cypraea diluculum
Distribution: Indo-Pacific to South Africa
Average size: 0.8 inch (2 cm)
Frequency: Locally common
Observations: Numerous subspecies

▼

Cypraeidae
Cypraea cribraria exmouthensis
Distribution: Western Australia, on coral
reefs and deep water
Average size: 1 inch (2.5 cm)
Frequency: Rare
Observations: Numerous subspecies

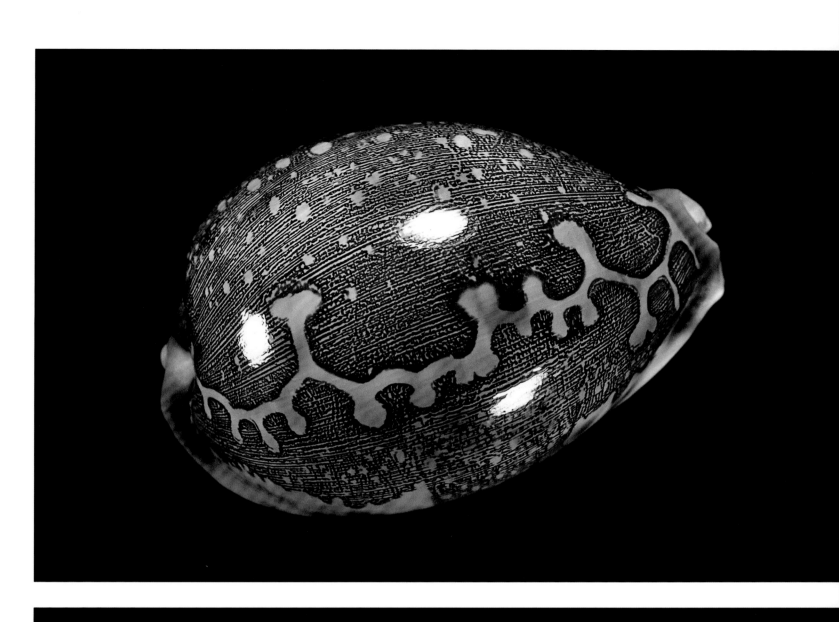

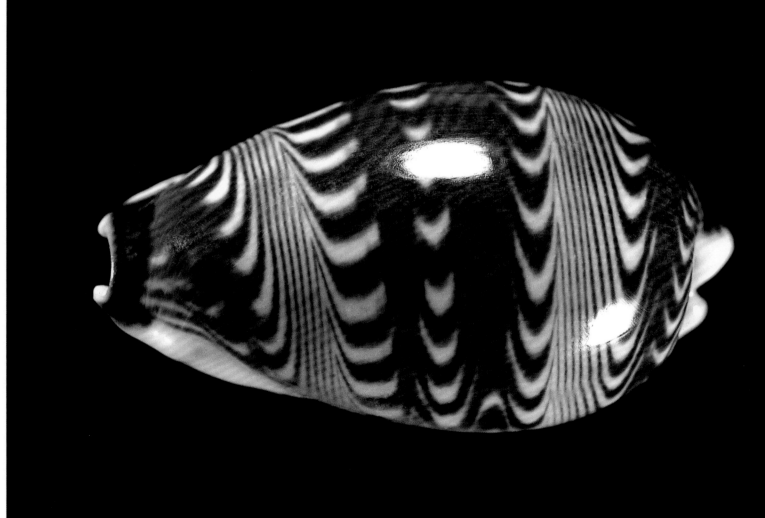

Cypraeidae
Cypraeovula cruickshanki
Distribution: Southern Africa, in deep water
Average size: 0.8 inch (2 cm)
Frequency: Very rare
Observations: Characteristically, a very
globular shape

Cypraeidae
Cypraeovula cruickshanki
Distribution: Southern Africa, in deep water
Average size: 0.8 inch (2 cm)
Frequency: Very rare
Observations: Characteristically, a very
globular shape

Cypraeidae
Cypraea granulata
Distribution: Hawaii
Average size: 0.8 inch (2 cm)
Frequency: Moderately rare
Observations: With *Cypraea nucleus*,
the only one to have a pustulose shell

Epitoniidae
Epitonium scalare
Distribution: Japan to the
southwestern Pacific
Average size: 2 inches (5 cm)
Frequency: Common

Epitoniidae
Epitonium rugosum
Distribution: The Philippines
Average size: 2.8 inches (7 cm)
Frequency: Uncommon

Fasciolariidae
Fusinus caparti
Distribution: Widely throughout Angola
Average size: 6 inches (15 cm)
Frequency: Locally common
Observations: Has been dredged down
to about 260 feet (80 m)

Fasciolariidae
Pleuroploca persica
Distribution: Indian Ocean, widely
distributed to a depth of 32 feet (10 m)
Average size: 4 inches (10 cm)
Frequency: Rare

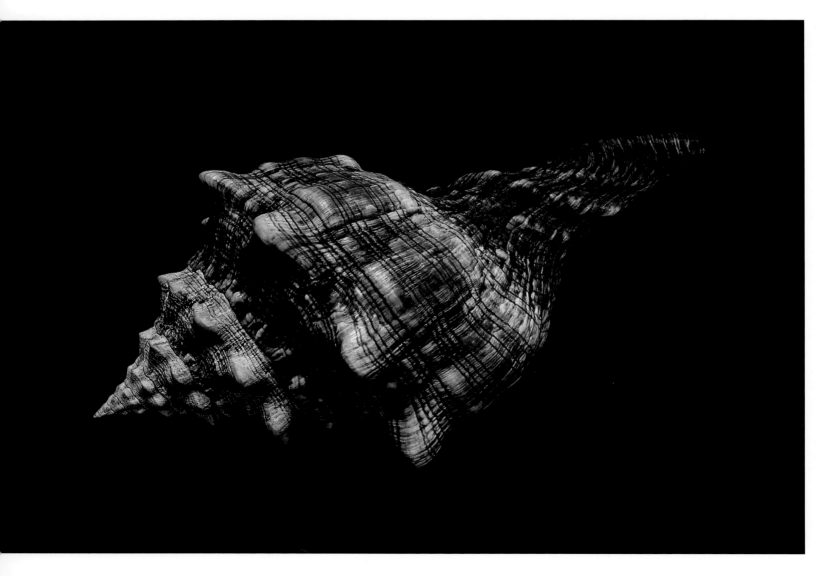

Fasciolariidae
Pleuroploca persica
Distribution: Indian Ocean, widely
distributed to a depth of 32 feet (10 m)
Average size: 4 inches (10 cm)
Frequency: Rare

Fasciolariidae
Opeatostoma pseudodon
Distribution: Western Mexico to Peru
Average size: 2 inches (5 cm)
Frequency: Common in shallow water
near rocks
Observations: Has a strong tooth near its
opening to open the bivalves it feeds on

Fasciolariidae
Opeatostoma pseudodon
Distribution: Western Mexico to Peru
Average size: 2 inches (5 cm)
Frequency: Common in shallow water
near rocks

Ficidae
Ficus investigatoris
Distribution: Indian Ocean in deep water
Average size: 2.4 inches (6 cm)
Frequency: Rare

Haliotitidae
Haliotis queketti
Distribution: KwaZulu Natal, South Africa,
in deep water, attached to rocks like other
Haliotitidae
Average size: 1.2 inches (3 cm)
Frequency: Rare

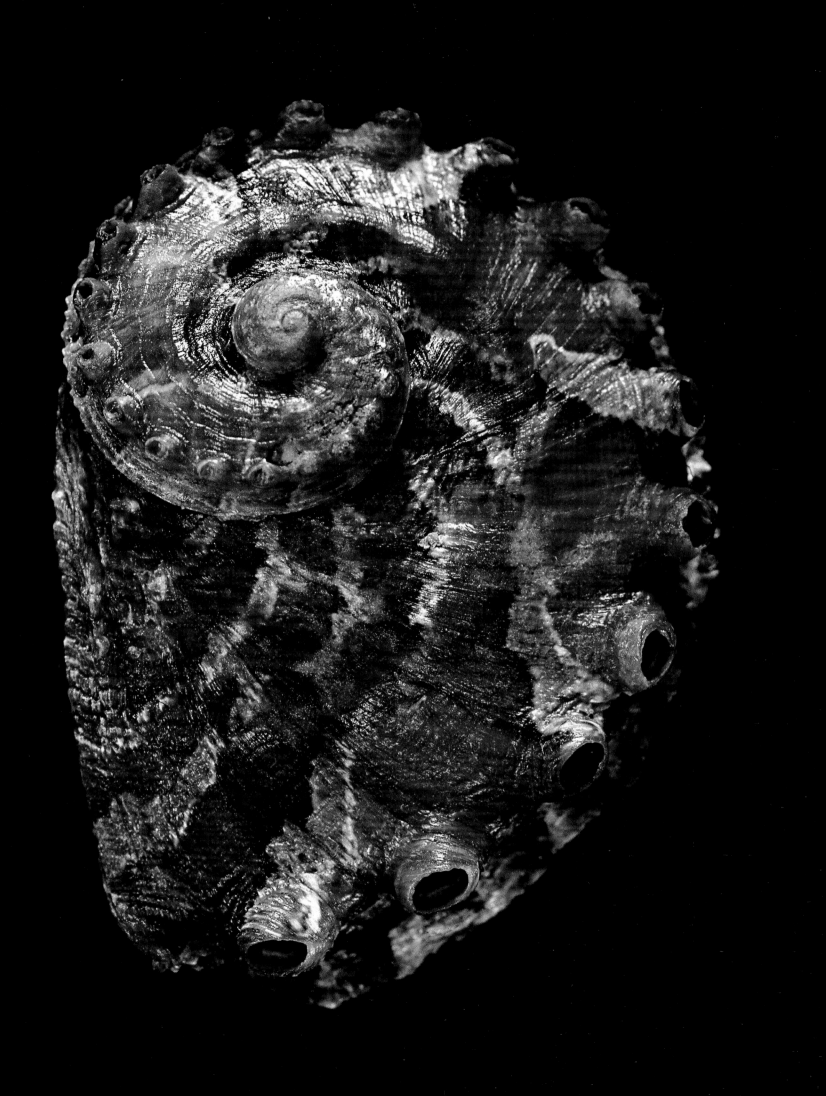

▶

Haliotitidae

Haliotis scalaris

Distribution: South and west Australia

Average size: 2.4 inches (6 cm)

Frequency: Uncommon

Observations: The beauty of this shell
is its deep ridges.

▼

Haliotitidae

Haliotis semistriata

Distribution: Indo-Pacific

Average size: 2.4 inches (6 cm)

Frequency: Common

Observations: Synonymous with
Haliotis varia

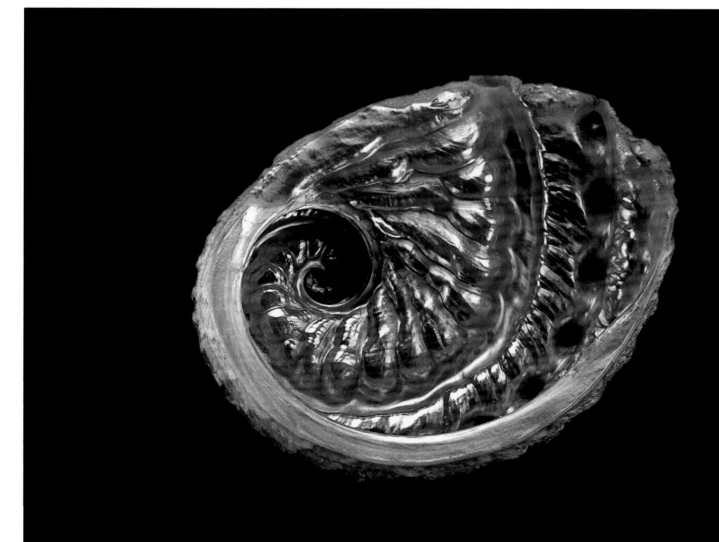

Haliotitidae

Haliotis asinina

Distribution: Southwestern Pacific

Average size: 2 inches (5 cm)

Frequency: Abundant

Observations: Capable of swimming for several feet using the wave motion of its mantle

Haliotitidae

Haliotis asinina

Distribution: Southwestern Pacific

Average size: 2 inches (5 cm)

Frequency: Abundant

Observations: Capable of swimming for several feet using the wave motion of its mantle

Haliotitidae

Haliotis asinina

Distribution: Southwestern Pacific

Average size: 2 inches (5 cm)

Frequency: Abundant

Observations: Capable of swimming for several feet using the wave motion of its mantle

Harpidae
Harpa harpa
Distribution: The entire Indo-Pacific
Average size: 2.4 inches (6 cm)
Frequency: Common

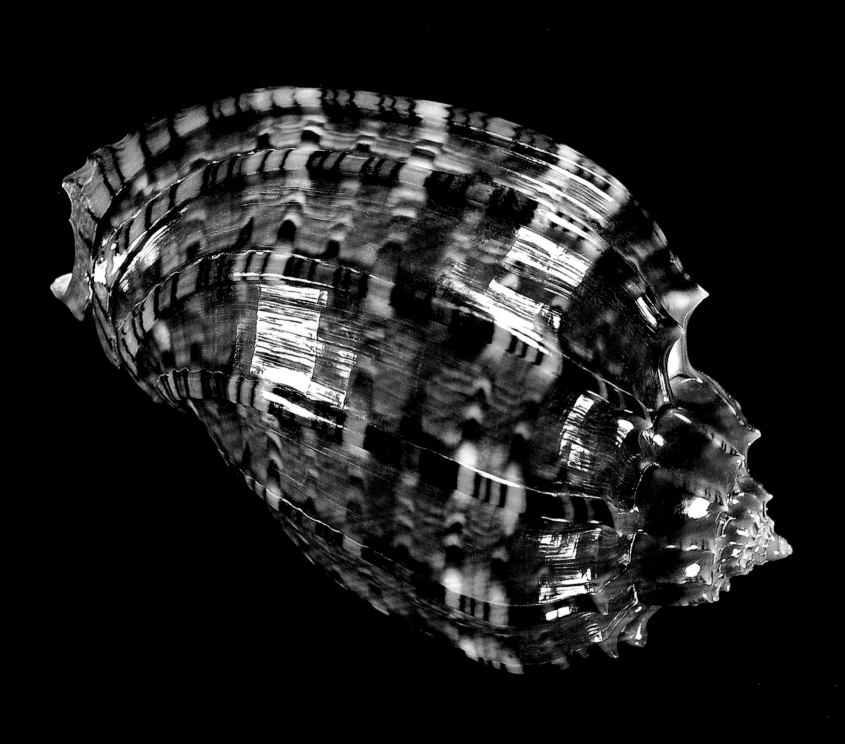

▶

Harpidae
Harpa cabriti
Distribution: Indian Ocean
Average size: 2 inches (5 cm)
Frequency: Relatively rare

Harpidae
Harpa costata
Distribution: Mauritius, southwest
Indian Ocean in shallow water
Average size: 2.8 inches (7 cm)
Frequency: Rare
Observations: Synonymous with
Harpa imperialis

▼

Harpidae
Austroharpa loisae
Distribution: Australia
Average size: 1 inch (2.5 cm)
Frequency: Rare, like all the *Austroharpa*

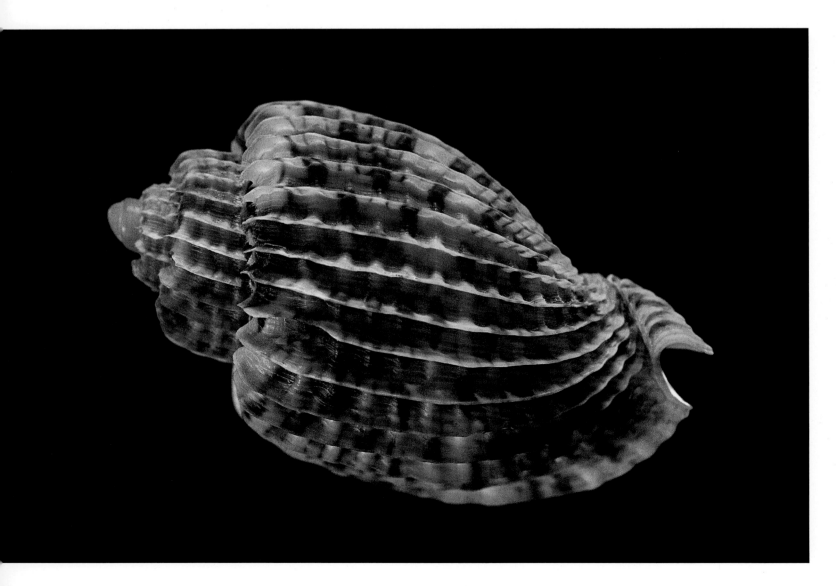

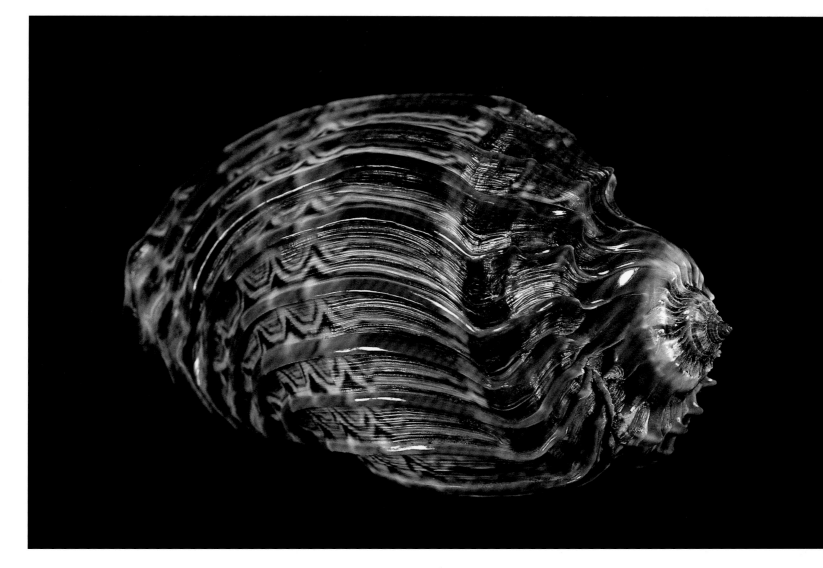

Hydatinidae
Hydatina nobilis
Distribution: Indo-Pacific
Average size: 0.8 inch (2 cm)
Frequency: Common
Observations: Synonymous with
Bullina lineata

Littorinidae
Tectarius pagodus
Distribution: Southwest Pacific, on
rocks above the tidal zone
Average size: 1.6 inches (4 cm)
Frequency: Common

Littorinidae
Littorina fasciata
Distribution: Western Mexico to the
Equator, on rocks in the intertidal zone
Average size: 1 inch (2.5 cm)
Frequency: Common

Marginellidae
Marginella strigata
Distribution: Southwest Asia, in
shallow water
Average size: 1.4 inches (3.5 cm)
Frequency: Uncommon

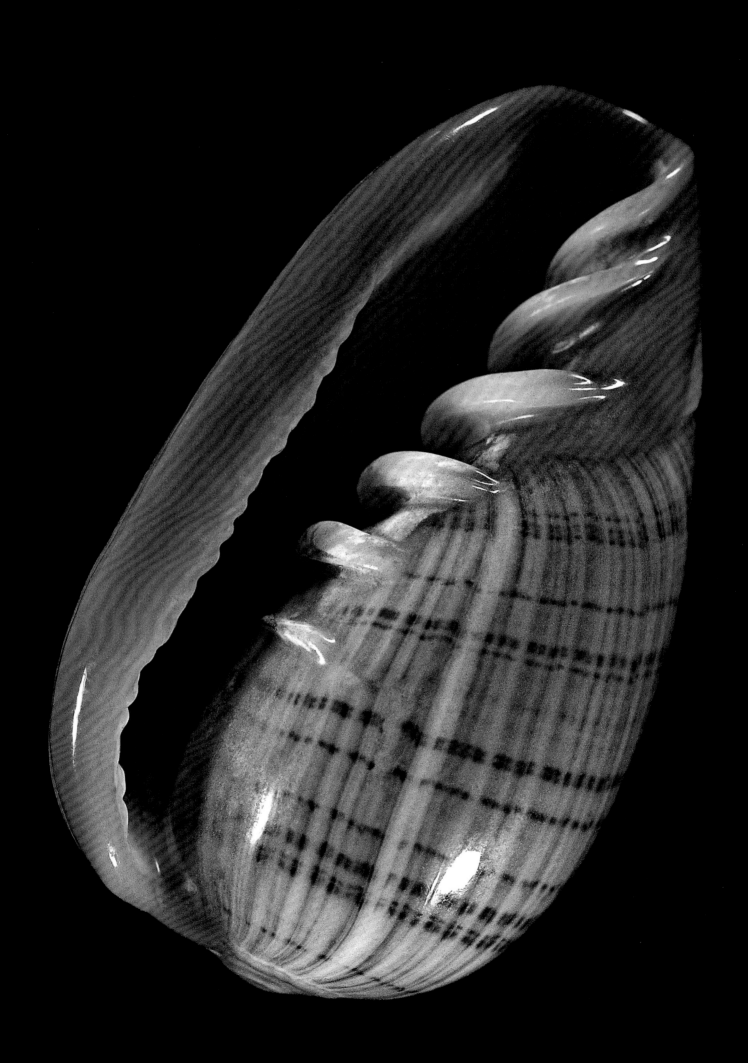

Mitridae
Mitra fusiformis zonata
Distribution: Atlantic Ocean, from the
Canary Islands to Morocco and in
the Mediterranean down to a depth
of 325 feet (100 m)
Average size: 2.8 inches (7 cm)
Frequency: Uncommon

▶

Mitridae

Mitra belcheri

Distribution: From the Gulf of California
to Panama

Average size: 4 inches (10 cm)

Frequency: Uncommon

Observations: Has been dredged down
to 325 feet (100 m)

▼

Mitridae

Cancilla filaris

Distribution: Indo-Pacific

Average size: 1 inch (2.5 cm)

Frequency: Common

Observations: Synonymous with

Cancilla filosa

Costellariidae
Vexillum citrinum
Distribution: Indo-Pacific
Average size: 2 inches (5 cm)
Frequency: Uncommon

Costellariidae
Vexillum sanguisugum
Distribution: Indo-Pacific
Average size: 1.6 inches (4 cm)
Frequency: Common

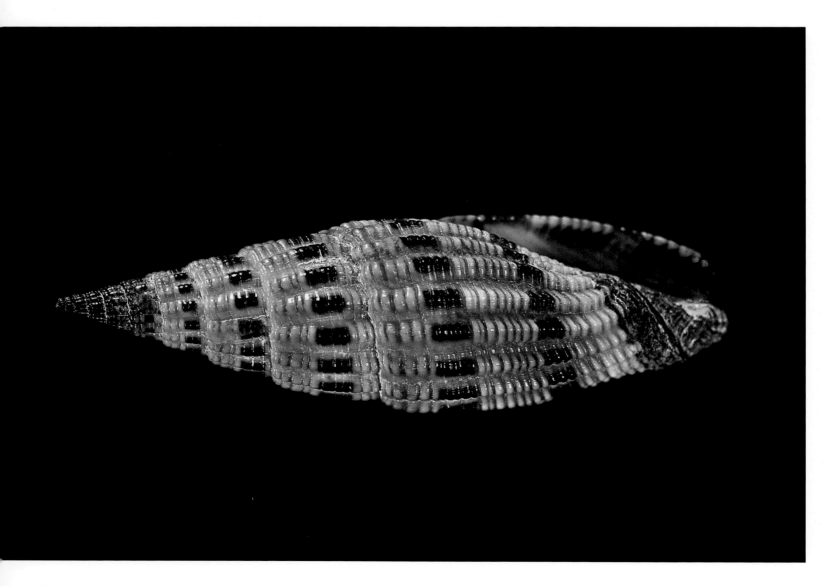

Costellariidae
Vexillum sanguisugum
Distribution: Indo-Pacific
Average size: 1.6 inches (4 cm)
Frequency: Common

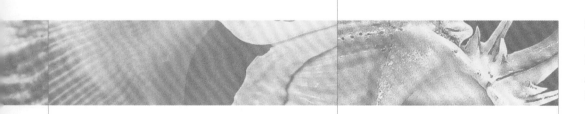

Muricidae
Siratus perelegans
Distribution: Western Atlantic
Average size: 1.8 inches (4.5 cm)
Frequency: Uncommon

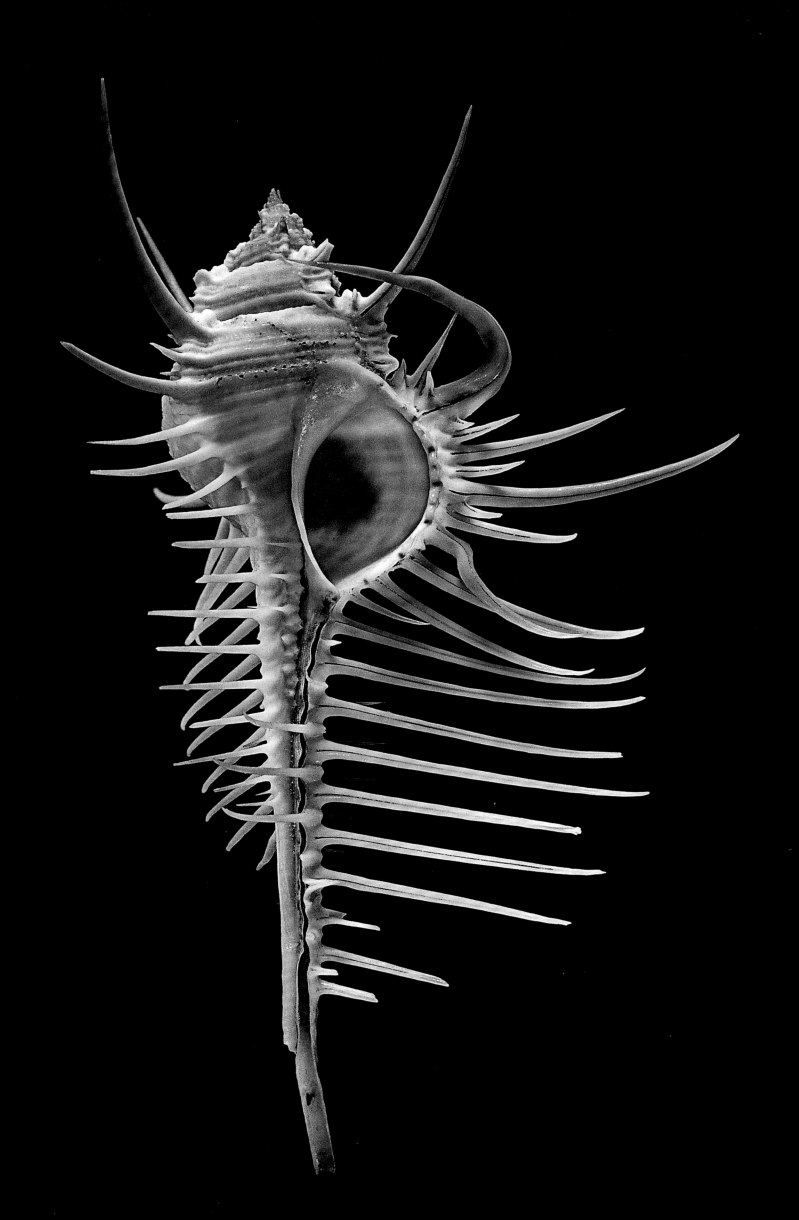

Muricidae
Pterynotus acanthopterus
Distribution: Western Australia
Average size: 2.4 inches (6 cm)
Frequency: Fairly common

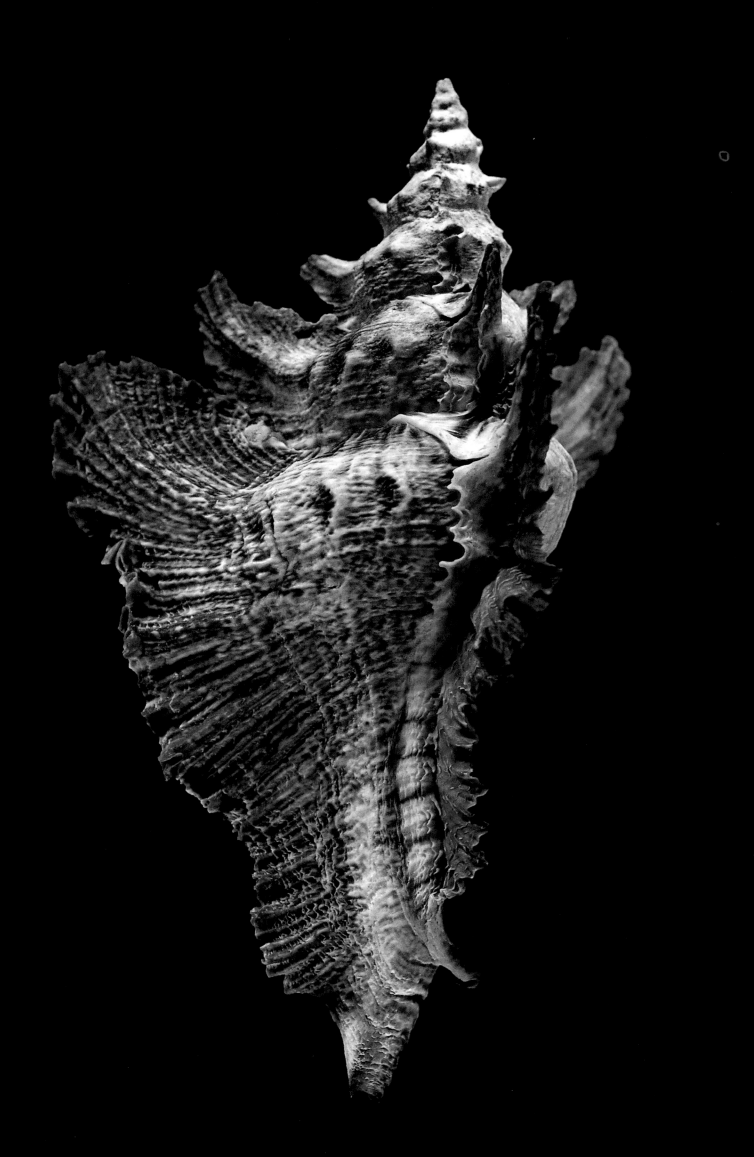

Muricidae
Ceratostoma burnetti
Distribution: Sea of Japan, Korea and
northern China, widely distributed to
a depth of 32 feet (10 m)
Average size: 3.1 inches (8 cm)
Frequency: Locally common

▶

Muricidae

Chicoreus cornucervi

Distribution: Northwest of Australia

Average size: 3.1 inches (8 cm)

Frequency: Uncommon

Observations: Not to be confused with

Chicoreus cervicornis

▼

Muricidae

Chicoreus cervicornis

Distribution: North of Australia

Average size: 2 inches (5 cm)

Frequency: Uncommon

Observations: Not to be confused with

Chicoreus cornucervi

▶

Muricidae

Siratus alabaster

Distribution: From the Philippines to
Japan, in deep water

Average size: 4 inches (10 cm)

Frequency: Locally common

▼

Muricidae

Oterynotuss orchidifloris

Distribution: Widely around Taiwan

Average size: 1.4 inches (3.5 cm)

Frequency: Uncommon

Observations: It is hard to find intact
spikes on this superb but fragile murex.

▶

Muricidae
Hexaplex cichoreus
Distribution: The Philippines
Average size: 3.1 inches (8 cm)
Frequency: Abundant
Observations: Synonymous with
Chicoreus endivia

Muricidae
Hexaplex cichoreus
Distribution: The Philippines
Average size: 3.1 inches (8 cm)
Frequency: Abundant
Observations: Synonymous with
Chicoreus endivia

▼

Muricidae
Homalocantha melanamathos chinii
Distribution: Widely in western Africa
Average size: 1 inch (2.5 cm)
Frequency: This subspecies is relatively rare.

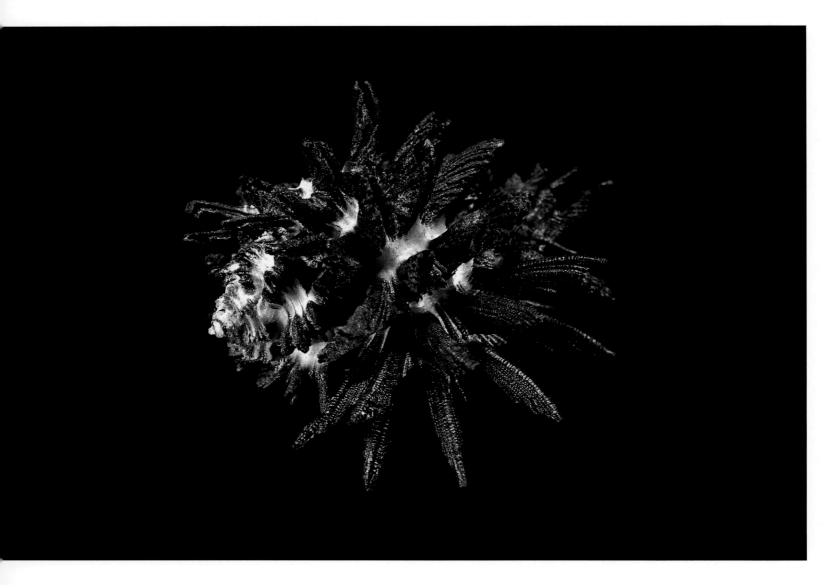

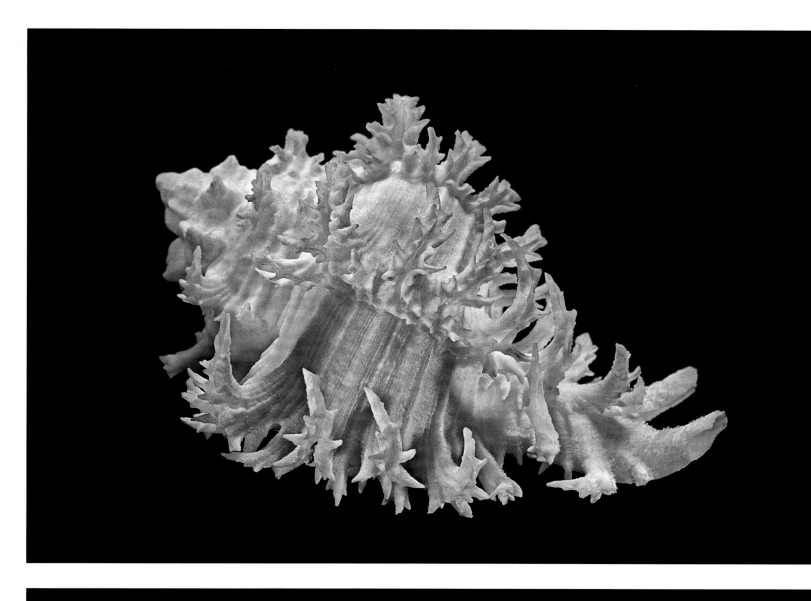

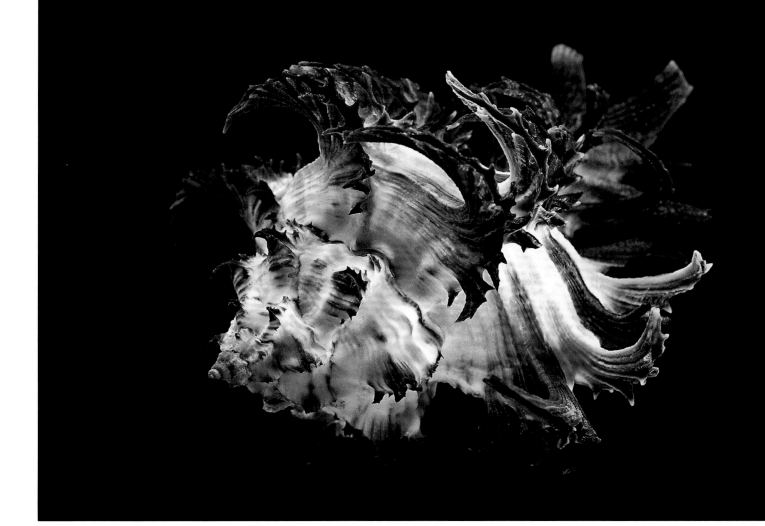

Muricidae
Trophon geversianus
Distribution: Western Atlantic
Average size: 2 inches (5 cm)
Frequency: Uncommon

Muricidae
Ceratostoma foliatum
Distribution: North America
Average size: 2.4 inches (6 cm)
Frequency: Uncommon

▼
Muricidae
Rapana bezoar
Distribution: Western Pacific, Japan
and Taiwan
Average size: 1.4 inches (3.5 cm)
Frequency: Common

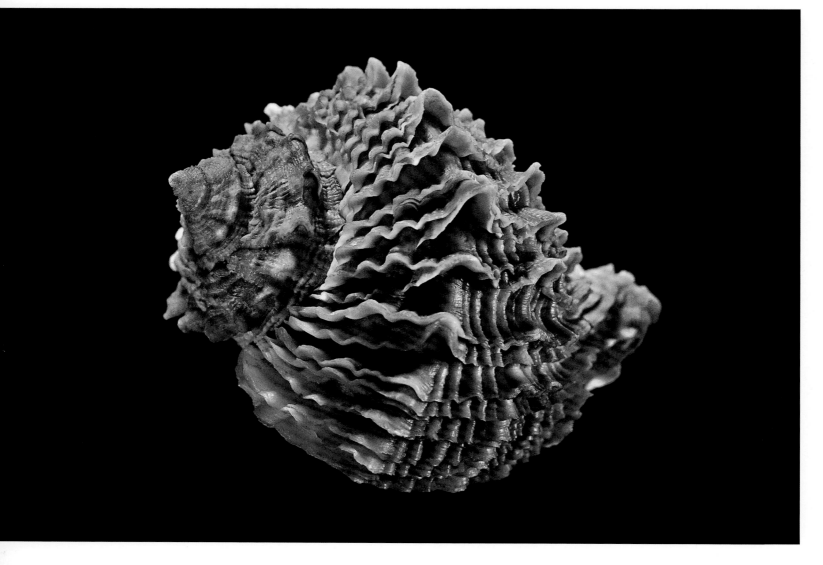

Muricidae
Pterynotus miyokoae
Distribution: Indo-Pacific
Average size: 2.4 inches (6 cm)
Frequency: Uncommon

►

Muricidae
Thais rugosa
Distribution: Indo-Pacific, India
and Singapore
Average size: 1.2 inches (3 cm)
Frequency: Common
Observations: Originally classified with
the Thaididae

▼

Muricidae
Pterynotus phyllopterus
Distribution: Guadeloupe
Average size: 2.4 inches (6 cm)
Frequency: Rare
Observations: A friend of the author, André
Lamy, who is a resident of Guadeloupe, has
bred these mollusks with excellent results;
they grow very well in aquaria and are in
better shape than those found by divers at
depths of 40–50 feet (12–15 m).

▶

Muricidae
Hexaplex regius
Distribution: Western Mexico to Peru
Average size: 4 inches (10 cm)
Frequency: Moderately common

▼

Muricidae
Phyllonotus brassica
Distribution: Western Mexico to Peru
Average size: 6.7 inches (17 cm)
Frequency: Relatively common

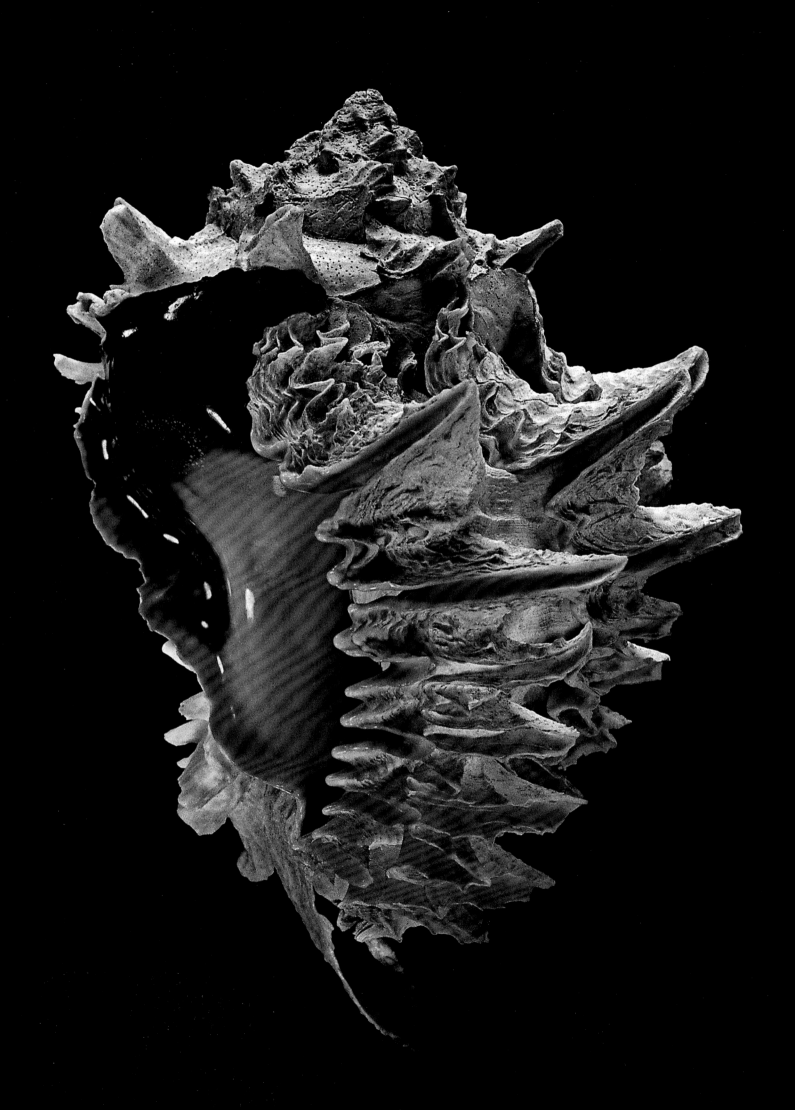

Muricidae

Haustellum haustellum

Distribution: Japan, western Australia, Red
Sea and Fiji

Average size: 4.7 inches (12 cm)

Frequency: Uncommon

Observations: Synonymous with *Murex
haustellum* and *Murex longicaudatum*

Muricidae
Haustellum hirasei
Distribution: Western Pacific, Philippines, Japan and Taiwan
Average size: 2.4 inches (6 cm)
Frequency: Uncommon

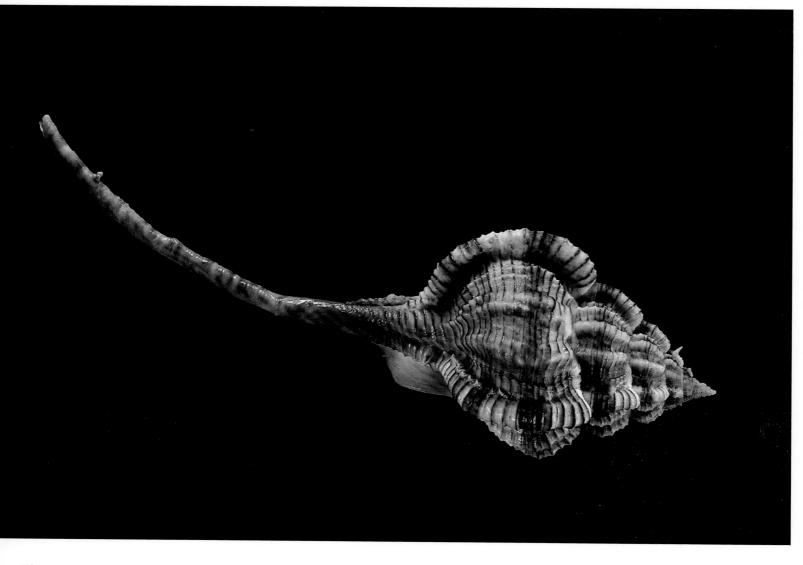

Muricidae
Murex tribulus
Distribution: Pacific, Red Sea
Average size: 2.8 inches (7 cm)
Frequency: Uncommon

Muricidae
Murex tribulus
Distribution: Pacific, Red Sea
Average size: 2.8 inches (7 cm)
Frequency: Uncommon

Muricidae
Homalocantha scorpio
Distribution: The Philippines
Average size: 1.4 inches (3.5 cm)
Frequency: Uncommon
Observations: Totally black or white
specimens are in great demand.

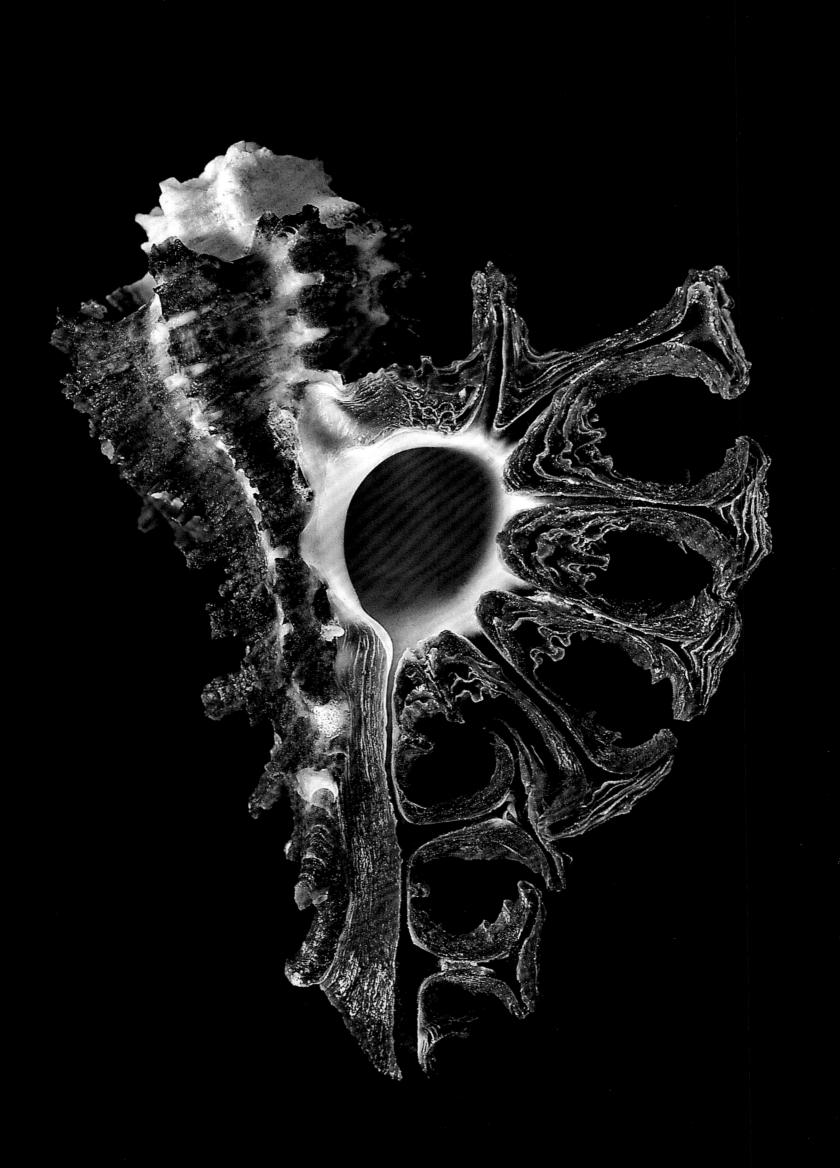

Muricidae
Chicoreus steeriae
Distribution: Marquesas Islands
Average size: 2 inches (5 cm)
Frequency: Uncommon

▼

Muricidae
Chicoreus sauliae
Distribution: Widely through the
southwest Pacific
Average size: 3.1 inches (8 cm)
Frequency: Uncommon

Muricidae
Chicoreus steeriae
Distribution: Marquesas Islands
Average size: 2 inches (5 cm)
Frequency: Uncommon

Muricidae
Drupa morum
Distribution: Indo-Pacific, on reefs in the
intertidal zone
Average size: 0.8 inch (2 cm)
Frequency: Common

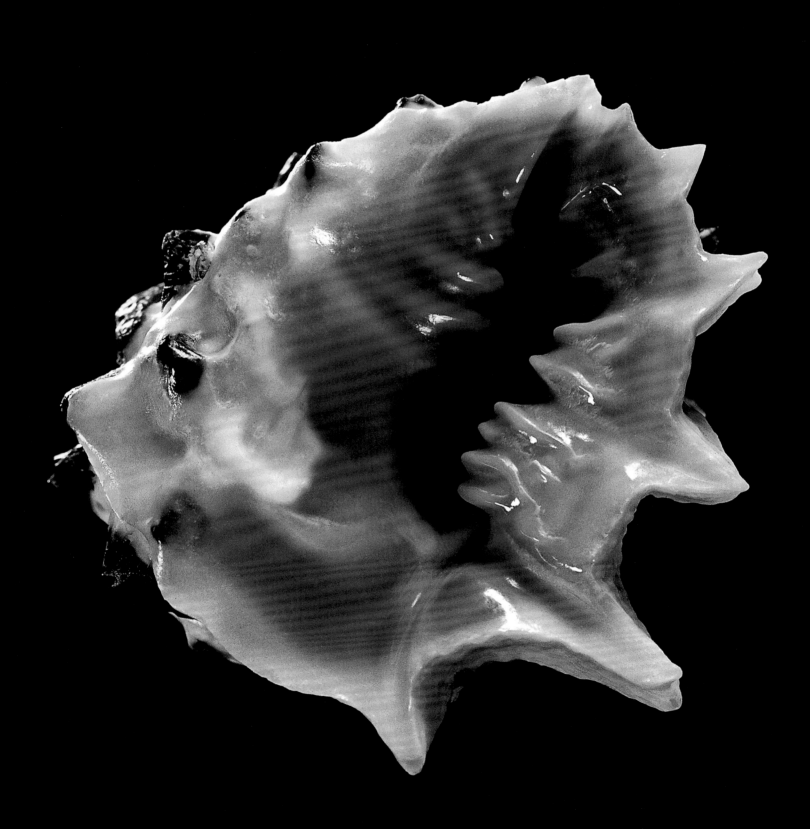

Neritidae
Nerita scabricostata
Distribution: Eastern Pacific
Average size: 1.4 inches (3.5 cm)
Frequency: Locally abundant
Observation: Like all neritas, this shell
needs to be accompanied by its
operculum to be identified.

Neritidae

Nerita exuvia

Distribution: Indo-Pacific oceans, on rocks or sand at the base of rocks

Average size: 0.5 inch (1.3 cm)

Frequency: Locally abundant

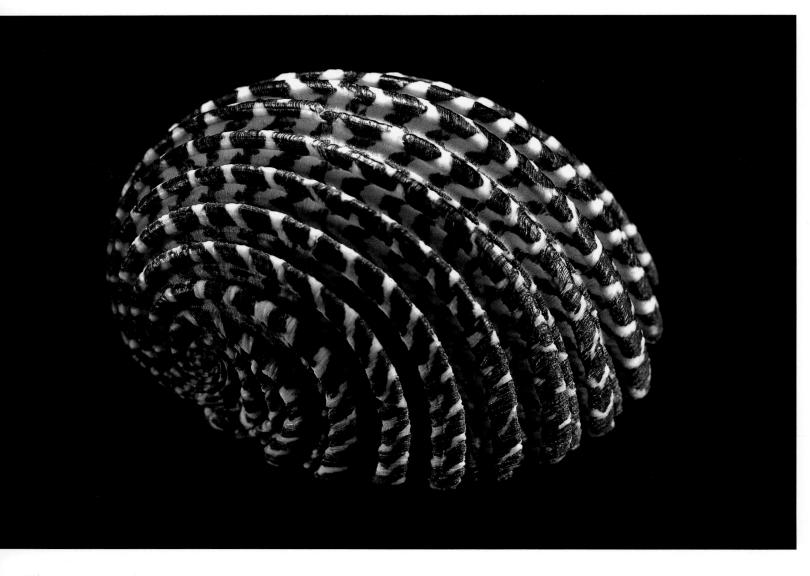

Neritidae
Nerita textilis
Distribution: Indo-Pacific
Average size: 1.2 inches (4 cm)
Frequency: Moderately common

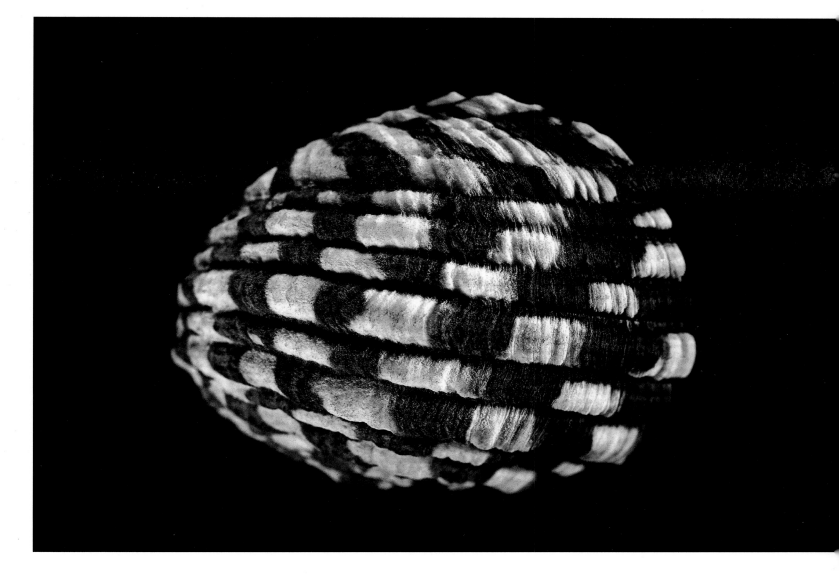

Neritidae
Neritina virginea
Distribution: Western Atlantic and Brazil, in the sand and algae washed ashore by the waves
Average size: 0.2 inch (6 mm)
Frequency: Locally abundant

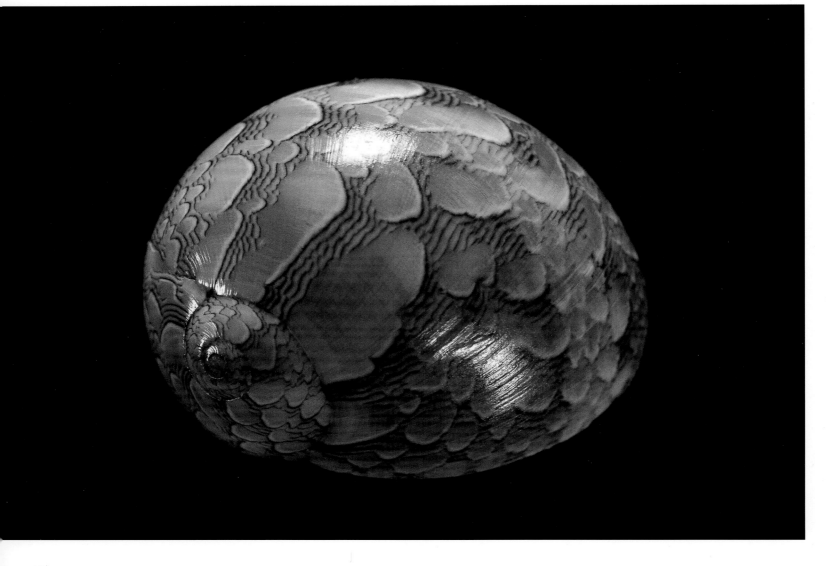

Neritidae
Neritina communis
Distribution: The Philippines, in the
sand and algae cast ashore by the waves
Average size: 0.5 inch (1.3 cm)
Frequency: Locally abundant

Neritidae
Neritina communis
Distribution: The Philippines, in the sand
and algae cast ashore by the waves
Average size: 0.5 inch (1.3 cm)
Frequency: Locally abundant

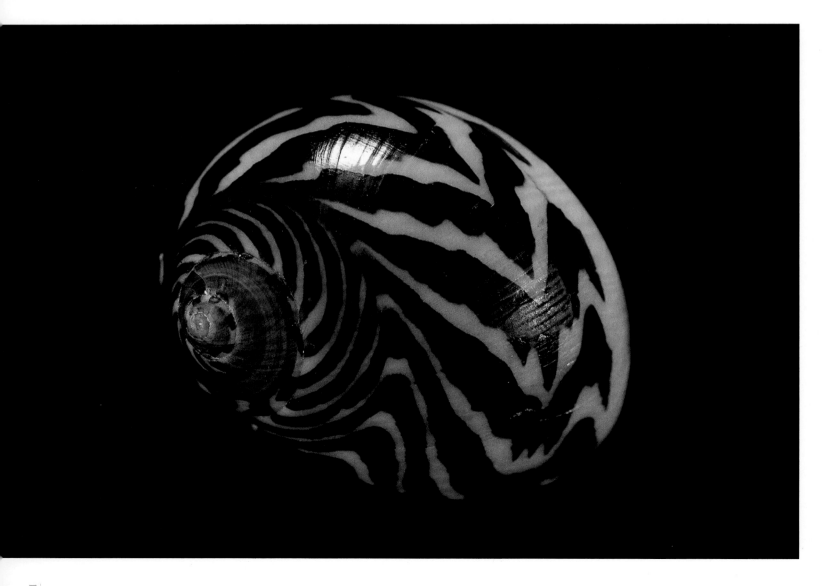

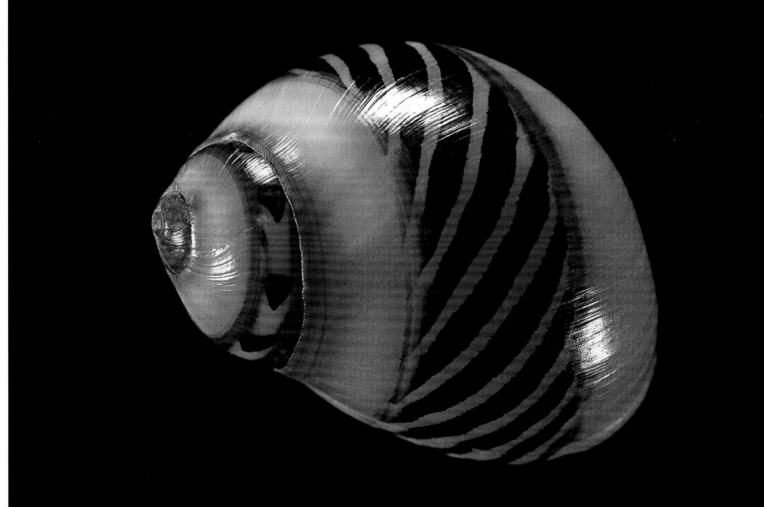

Neritopsidae
Neritopsis radula
Distribution: Indo-Pacific, in shallow
water near reefs
Average size: 1.4 inches (3.5 cm)
Frequency: Uncommon

Olividae

Melapium elatum

Distribution: Southern Africa and
Mozambique

Average size: 1.8 inches (4.5 cm)

Frequency: Very rare except for dead
specimens collected on beaches and
in shallow water

Observations: Rarely found alive

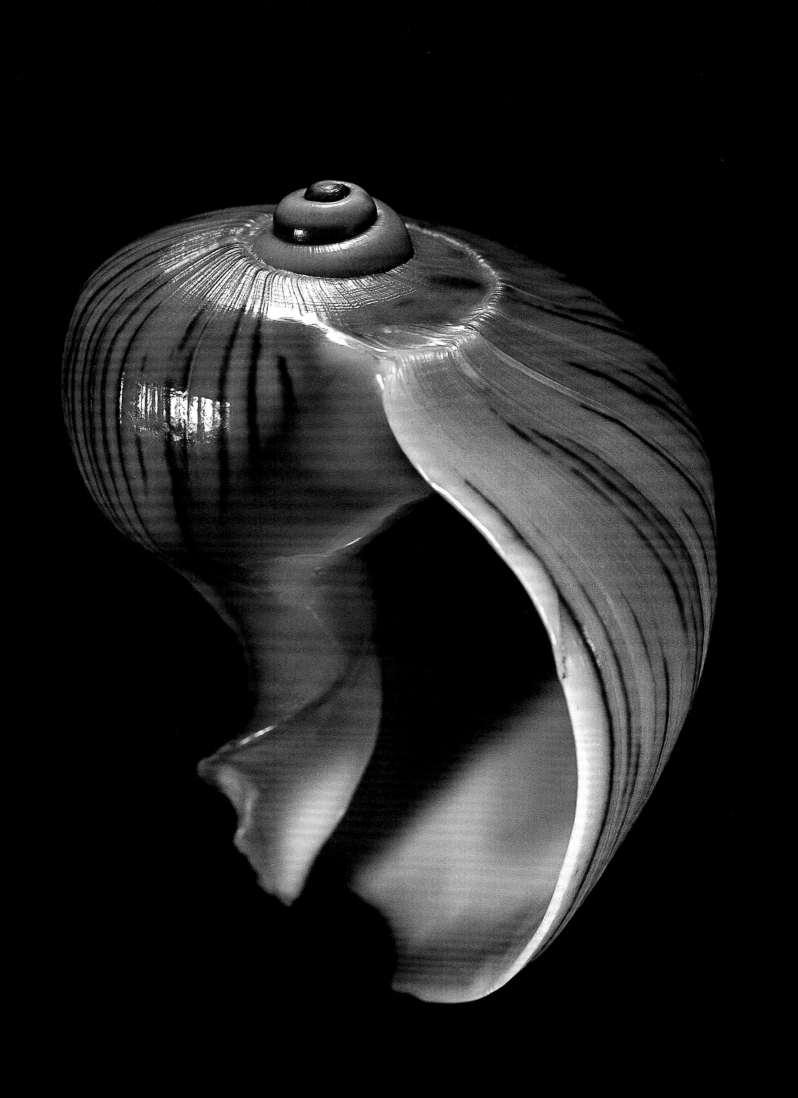

▶

Olividae

Ancilla lienardi

Distribution: Brazil, in damp sand and
shallow water
Average size: 1.6 inches (4 cm)
Frequency: Fairly common

▼

Olividae

Oliva oliva

Distribution: Indo-Pacific
Average size: 0.8 inch (2 cm)
Frequency: Locally abundant
Observations: At low tide you can follow
their cordlike tracks in the sand, which can
reach lengths of 16–20 feet (5–6 m).

Olividae

Olivancillaria gibbosa

Distribution: Indian Ocean
Average size: 1.8 inches (4.5 cm)
Frequency: Locally abundant
Observations: At low tide you can follow
their cordlike tracks in the sand, which can
reach lengths of 16–20 feet (5–6 m).

Olividae

Ancillista velesiana

Distribution: Western Australia, in damp
sand and shallow water
Average size: 3.1 inches (8 cm)
Frequency: Uncommon

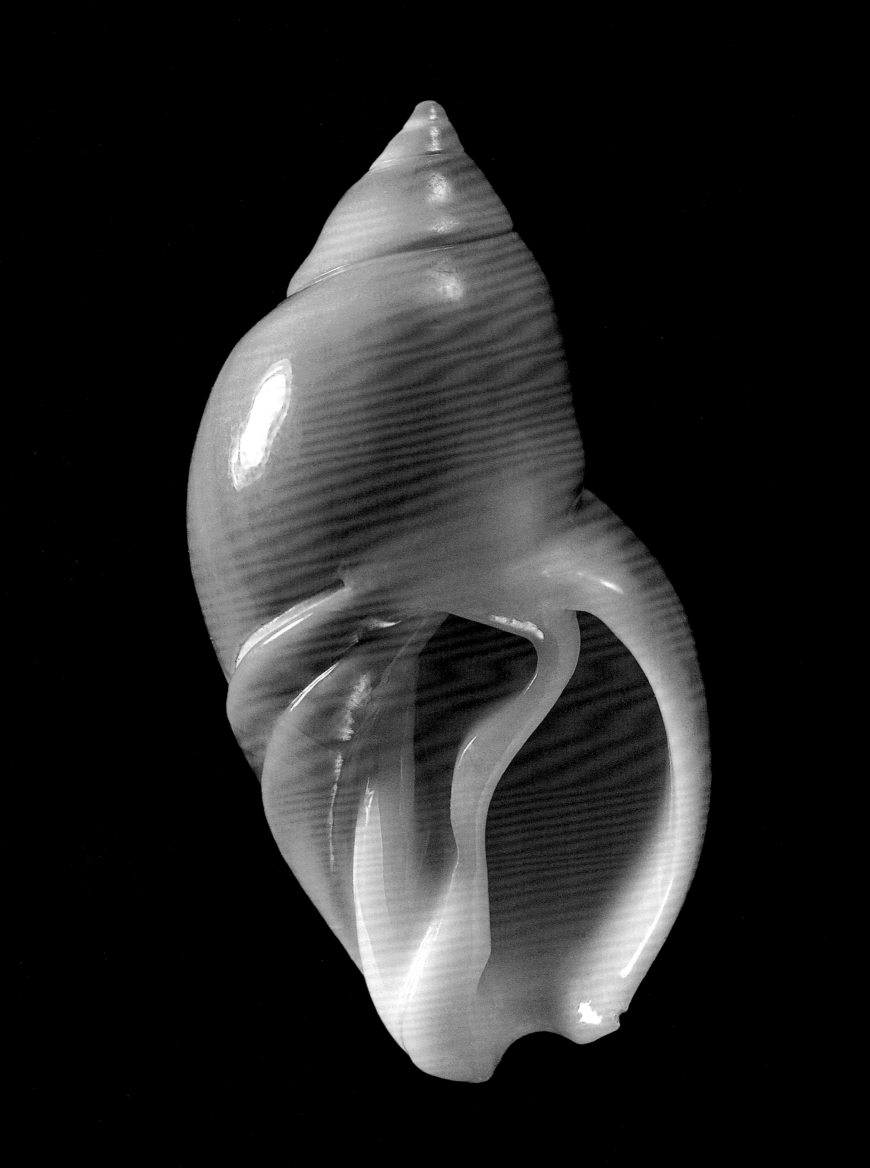

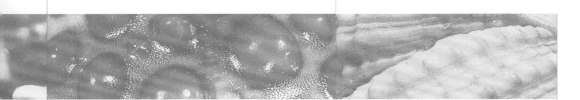

Ovulidae
Jenneria pustulata
Distribution: From California to the Equator,
near large coral in shallow water
Average size: 0.8 inch (2 cm)
Frequency: Moderately common

Ovulidae
Calpurnus verrucosus
Distribution: Indo-Pacific
Average size: 1 inch (2.5 cm)
Frequency: Locally common
Observations: Abundant on some
underwater canyons in shallow water

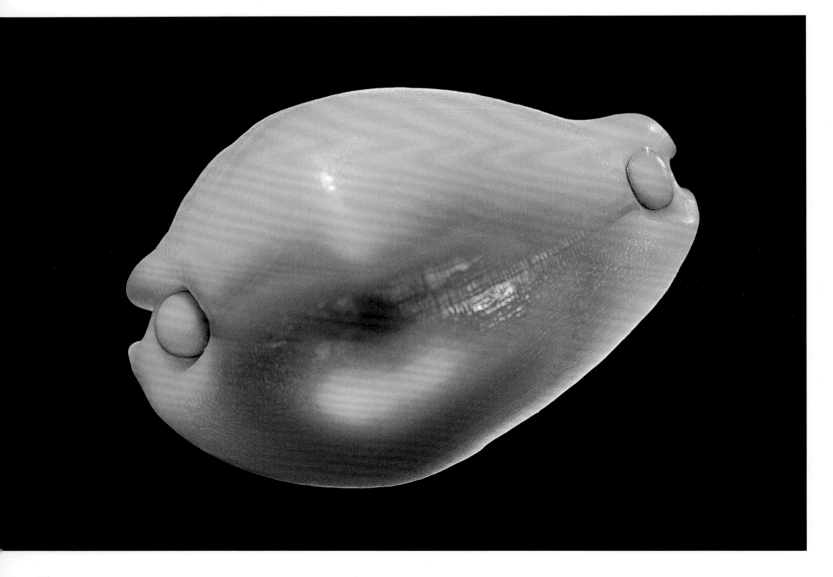

▶

Ovulidae
Margovula pyriformis
Distribution: Australia and Papua
New Guinea
Average size: 0.6 inch (1.6 cm)
Frequency: Relatively common

▼

Ovulidae
Volva volva habei
Distribution: Indo-Pacific
Average size: 4 inches (10 cm)
Frequency: Fairly common

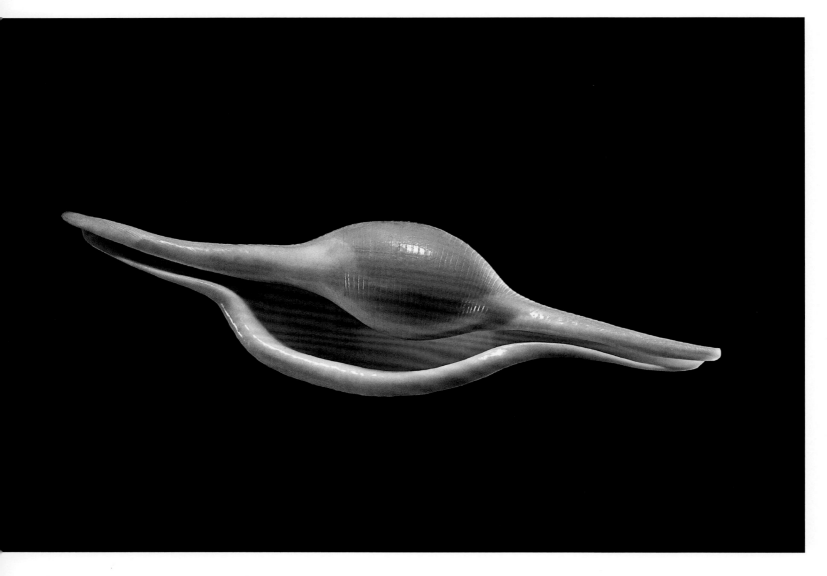

Personidae
Distorsio perdistorta
Distribution: Caribbean, Japan and
Madagascar in deep waters
Average size: 2 inches (5 cm)
Frequency: Uncommon

▶

Personidae
Distorsio decipiens
Distribution: The Philippines
Average size: 2 inches (5 cm)
Frequency: Fairly common

▼

Personidae
Distorsio kurzi
Distribution: Central Philippines, in
deep water
Average size: 1.2 inches (3 cm)
Frequency: Uncommon

Personidae
Distorsio anus ▶▶
Distribution: Indo-Pacific, under coral
in shallow water
Average size: 2.4 inches (6 cm)
Frequency: Uncommon

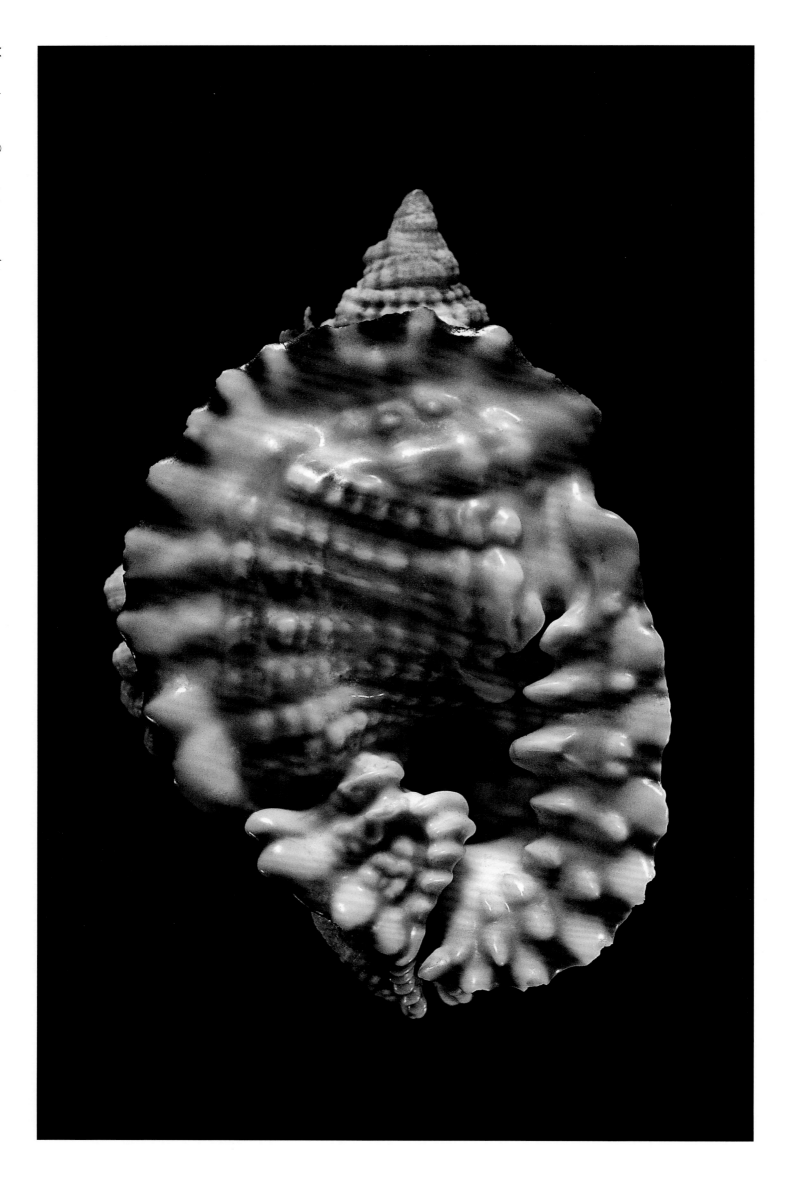

Phasianellidae
Phasianella australis
Distribution: South Australia and Tasmania
Average size: 2 inches (5 cm)
Frequency: Common
Observations: Solid calcareous operculum

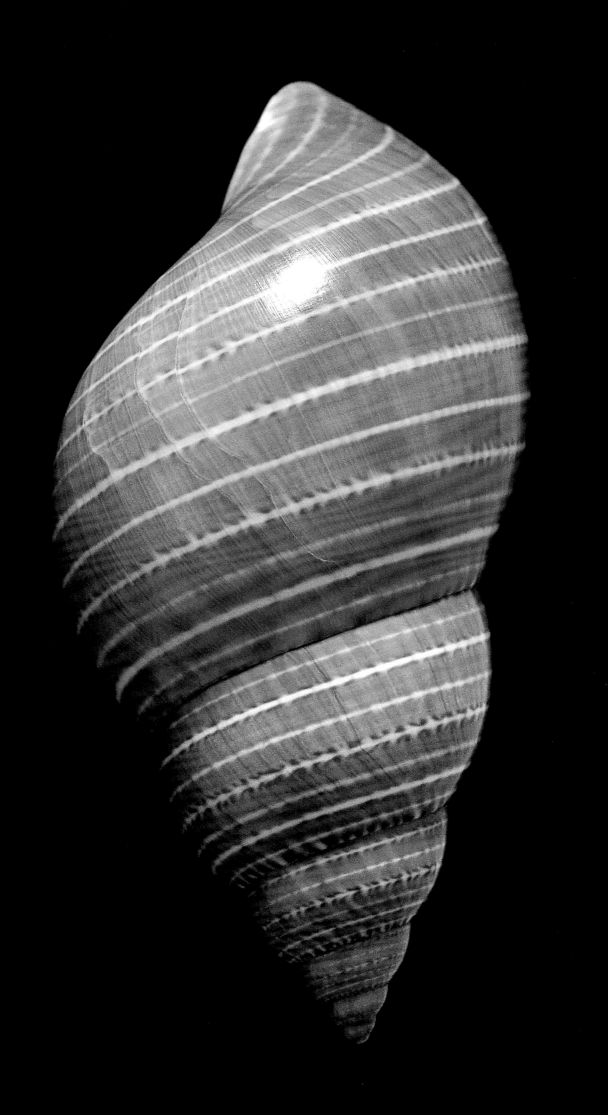

Phasianellidae
Phasianella australis
Distribution: South Australia and Tasmania
Average size: 2 inches (5 cm)
Frequency: Common
Observations: Solid calcareous operculum

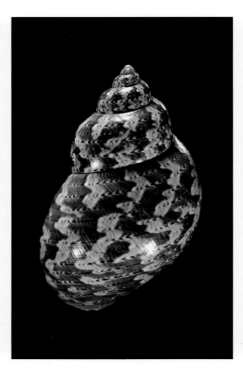
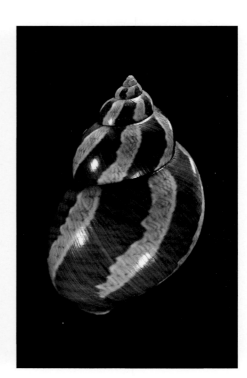

Phasianellidae
Phasianella australis
Distribution: South Australia and Tasmania
Average size: 2 inches (5 cm)
Frequency: Common
Observations: Solid calcareous operculum

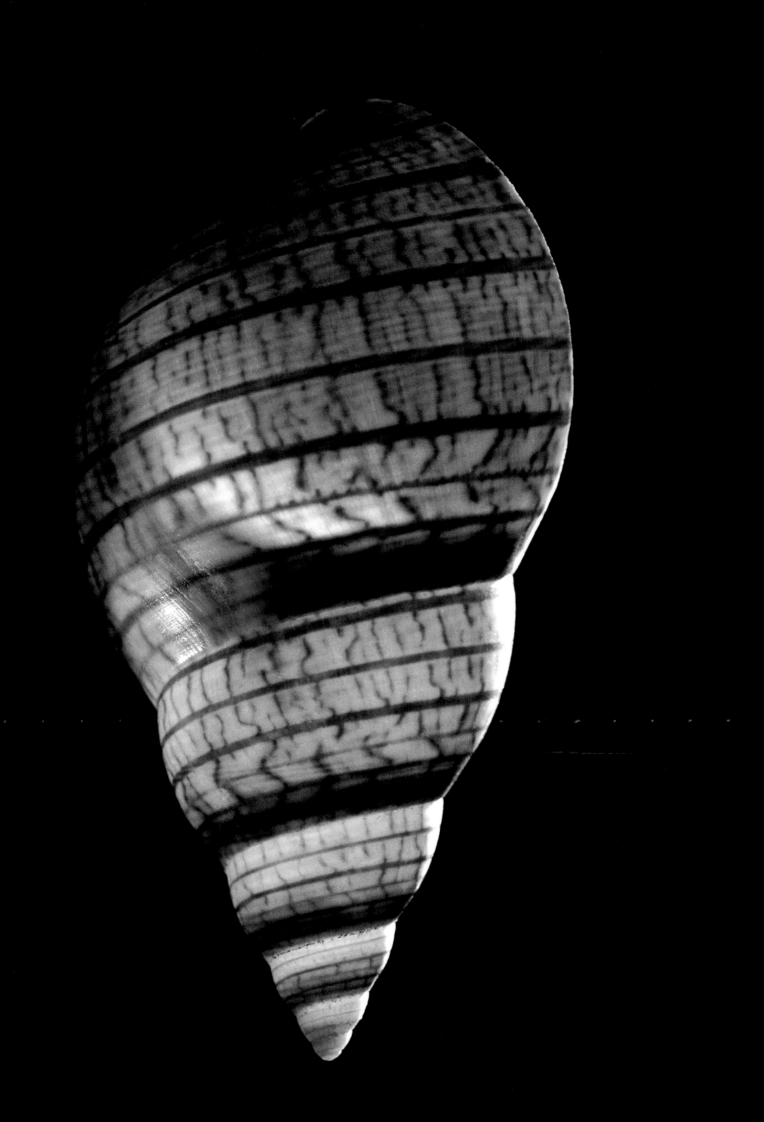

Pleurotomariidae
Perotrochus vicdani
Distribution: The Philippines, deeper than
325 feet (100 m)
Average size: 2.4 inches (6 cm)
Frequency: Rare

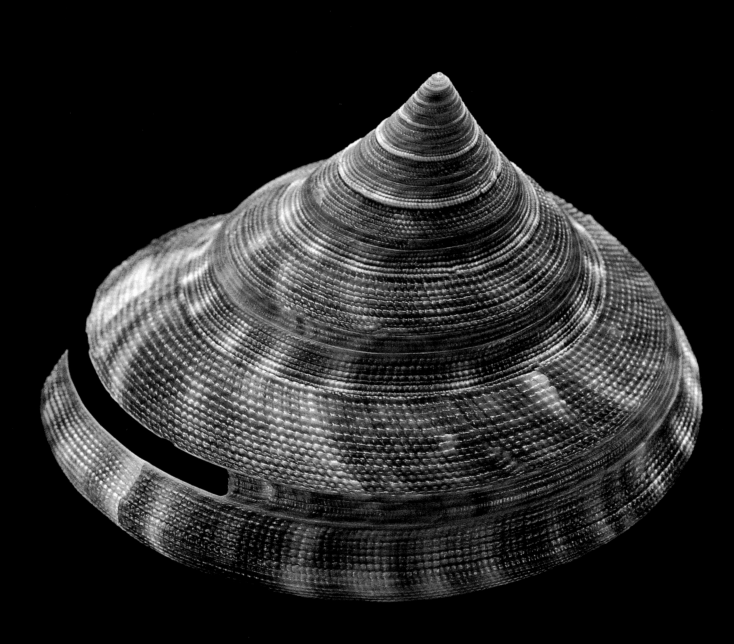

Ranellidae
Cymatium perryi
Distribution: Widely near Sri Lanka and
southern India
Average size: 3.1 inches (8 cm)
Frequency: Uncommon

Ranellidae
Charonia tritonis (triton)
Distribution: Indo-Pacific, in shallow-water
coral reefs
Average size: 10 inches (25 cm)
Frequency: Moderately common

Ranellidae
Cymatium lotorium ▸▸
Distribution: Tropical Indo-Pacific, in shallow
water near coral reefs
Average size: 3.1 inches (8 cm)
Frequency: Uncommon

▶

Ranellidae
Cymatium hepaticum
Distribution: Tropical Indo-Pacific,
under coral beds
Average size: 1.2 inches (4 cm)
Frequency: Uncommon

▼

Ranellidae
Galegna clandestina
Distribution: Western Pacific,
widely distributed
Average size: 1.2 inches (4 cm)
Frequency: Uncommon
Observations: Synonymous with
Galegna succinta

Ranellidae
Biplex perca
Distribution: The Philippines and Australia
Average size: 1.6 inches (4 cm)
Frequency: Moderately common
Observations: A large but very flat shell

Siliquariidae
Siliquaria ponderosa
Distribution: Southwestern Pacific,
in shallow water
Average size: 6 inches (15 cm)
Frequency: Uncommon
Observations: Unlinked spires

Siliquariidae
Siliquaria anguina
Distribution: Western Pacific
Average size: 5.1 inches (13 cm)
Frequency: Uncommon
Observations: Unlinked spires

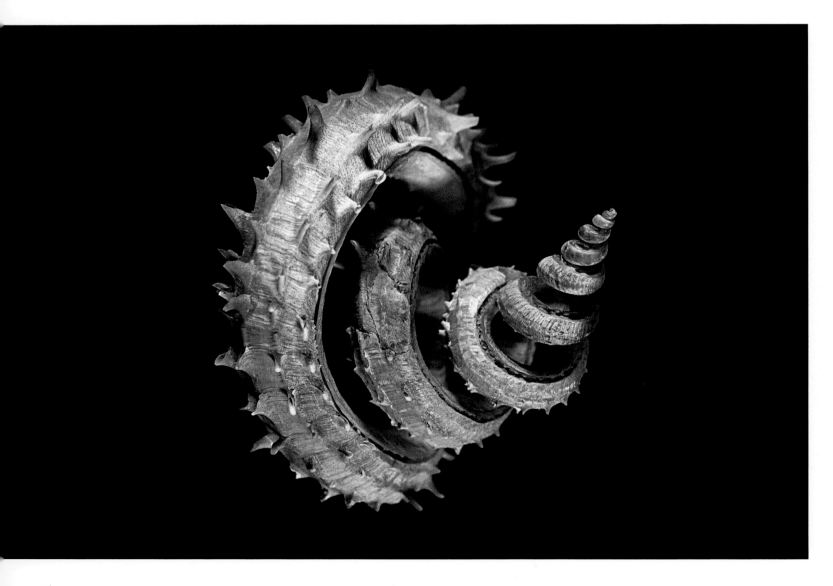

Siliquariidae
Siliquaria anguina
Distribution: Western Pacific
Average size: 5.1 inches (13 cm)
Frequency: Uncommon
Observations: Unlinked spires

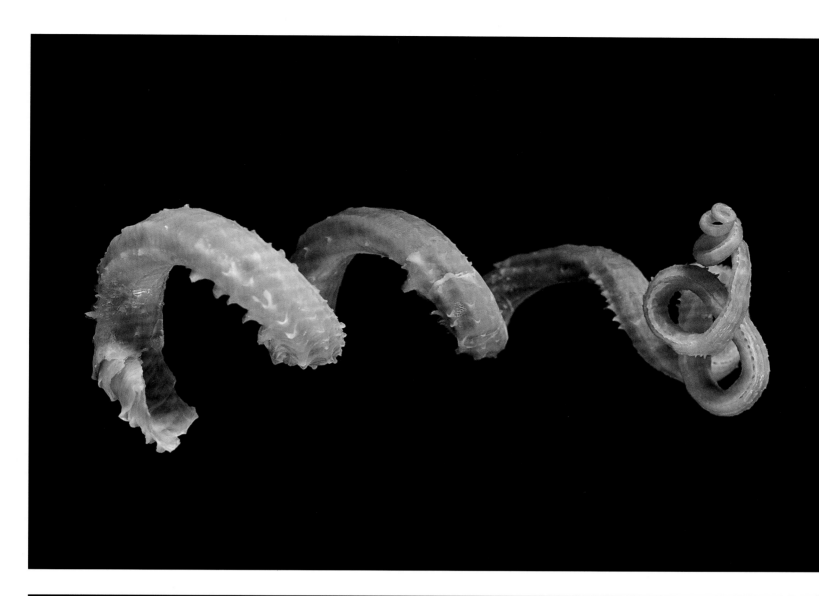

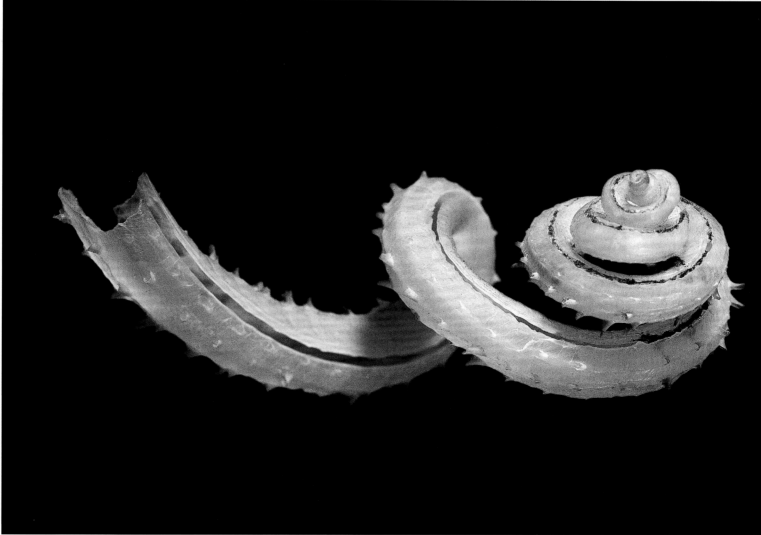

Strombidae
Lambis digitata
Distribution: Indo-Pacific
Average size: 4 inches (10 cm)
Frequency: Uncommon
Observations: Synonymous with
Lambis elongate

Strombidae
Lambis lambis
Distribution: Indo-Pacific
Average size: 6.3 inches (16 cm)
Frequency: Common
Observations: The females' digitations are longer than those of males.

Strombidae
Lambis lambis ▶▶
Distribution: Indo-Pacific
Average size: 6.3 inches (16 cm)
Frequency: Common
Observations: The females' digitations are longer than those of males.

Strombidae
Lambis chiragra arthritica
Distribution: Eastern Africa, on reefs in
shallow water
Average size: 5.1 inches (13 cm)
Occurrence: Common

Tibia insulaechorab ▸▸
Distribution: Indian Ocean, from the
intertidal zone to moderate depths
Average size: 4.7 inches (12 cm)
Frequency: Common

▶

Strombidae

Tibia fusus melanocheilus

Distribution: The Philippines and Indonesia, in
shallow water

Average size: 5.1 inches (13 cm)

Occurrence: Uncommon

▼

Strombidae

Tibia martini

Distribution: The Philippines, Taiwan and
Indonesia, in deep water

Average size: 4.7 inches (12 cm)

Frequency: Fairly rare

Strombidae

Strombus vomer iredalei

Distribution: North of Australia

Average size: 2.4 inches (6 cm)

Occurrence: Uncommon

Observations: Synonymous with *Strombus australis*

Strombidae

Tibia powisi

Distribution: Southwest Pacific Ocean
and Australia

Average size: 2 inches (5 cm)

Frequency: Uncommon

Observations: Dredged in moderately
deep water

Strombidae
Rimella cancellata
Distribution: The Philippines and Thailand
Average size: 1.2 inches (4 cm)
Occurrence: Locally common

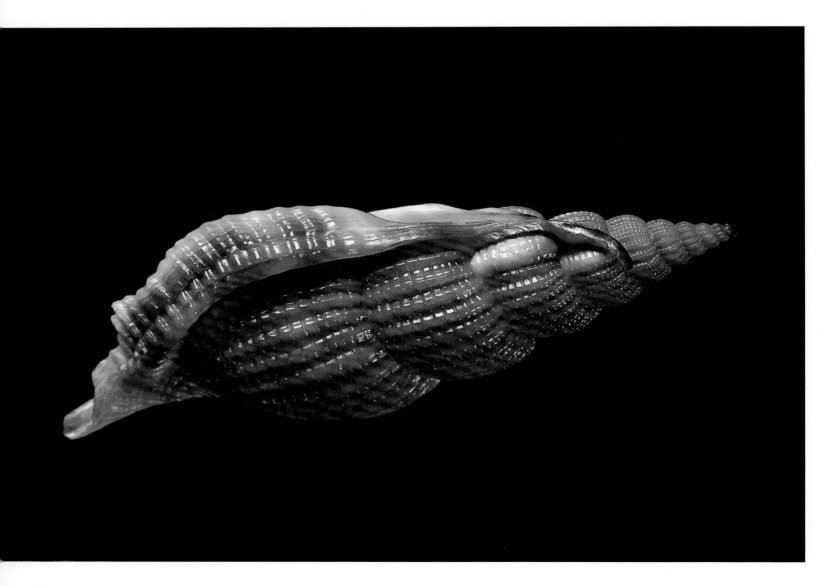

Strombidae
Rimella cancellata
Distribution: The Philippines and Thailand
Average size: 1.2 inches (4 cm)
Occurrence: Locally common

Strombidae
Strombus listeri
Distribution: Northwest Indian Ocean
and the Bay of Bengal, in moderately
deep water
Average size: 4.3 inches (11 cm)
Occurrence: Uncommon

Strombidae
Strombus listeri
Distribution: Northwest Indian Ocean
and the Bay of Bengal, in moderately
deep water
Average size: 4.3 inches (11 cm)
Occurrence: Uncommon

▶

Strombidae
Strombus vittatus vittatus
Distribution: South China Sea as far as Fiji,
widely distributed
Average size: 2.8 inches (7 cm)
Occurrence: Uncommon

▼

Strombidae
Strombus gibberulus albus
Distribution: Red Sea and the Gulf of
Aden, from the intertidal zone to a
depth of 32 feet (10 m)
Average size: 1.2 inches (4 cm)
Occurrence: Moderately common

Strombidae
Strombus goliath
Distribution: Endemic to Brazil, found
on beaches
Average size: 12 inches (30 cm)
Occurrence: Uncommon

▼
Strombidae
Strombus gigas
Distribution: Southeast of Florida, Bermuda,
West Indies
Average size: 7.1 inches (18 cm)
Occurrence: Common but in danger of
being overfished

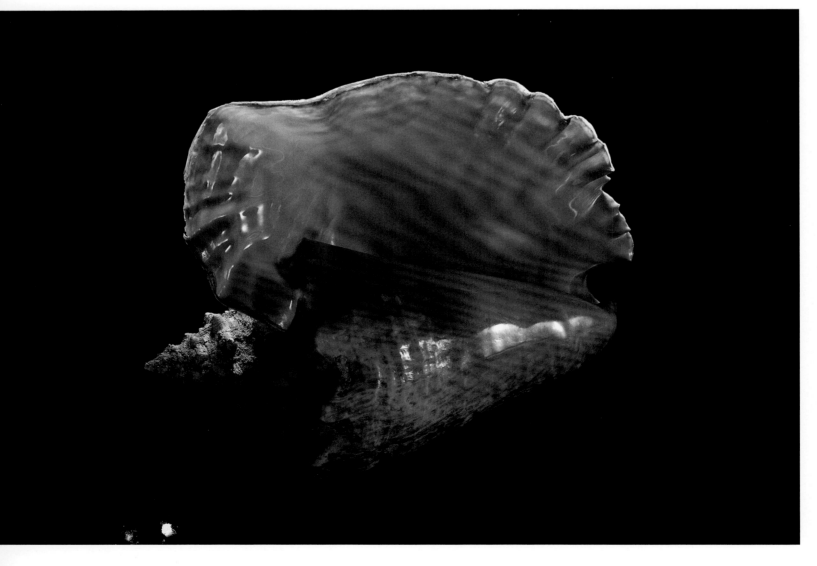

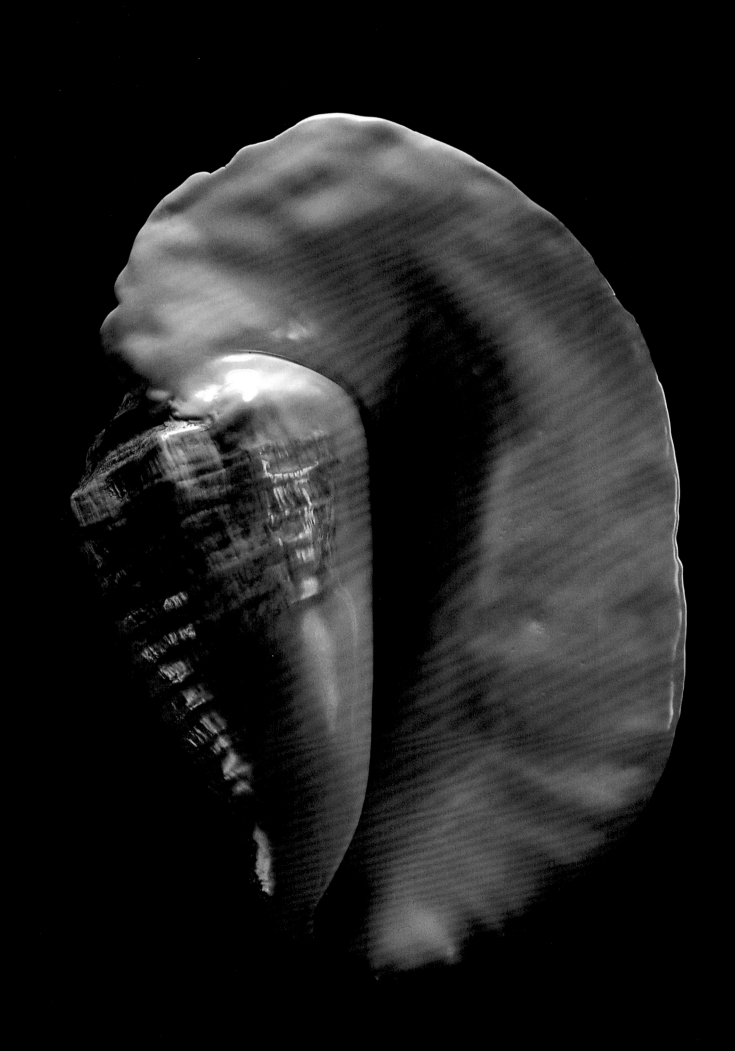

Turritellidae
Turritella terebra
Distribution: Southwest Pacific Ocean
Average size: 5.5 inches (14 cm)
Frequency: Locally abundant
Observations: Found at low tide in the sand
and mud

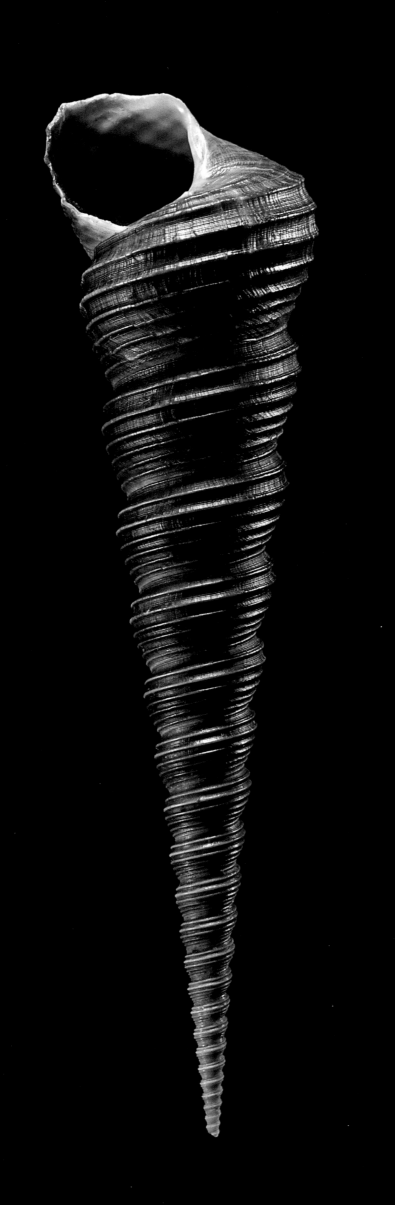

Terebridae
Terebra dimidiata
Distribution: Indo-Pacific, in sand and
shallow water
Average size: 4.3 inches (11 cm)
Frequency: Common

Terebridae
Terebra dimidiata
Distribution: Indo-Pacific, in sand and
shallow water
Average size: 4.3 inches (11 cm)
Frequency: Common

Terebridae
Terebra duplicata
Distribution: The western Indo-Pacific, in
sand and shallow water
Average size: 1.7 inches (4.5 cm)
Frequency: Common

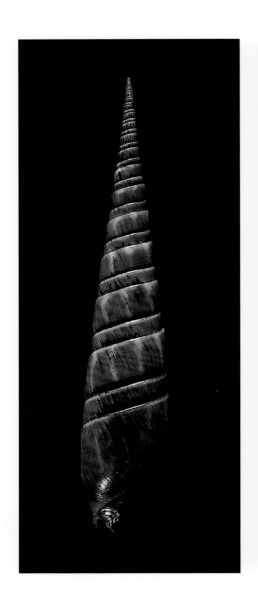
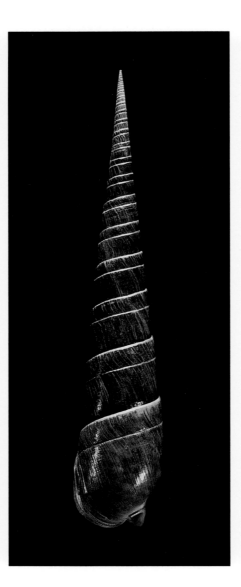
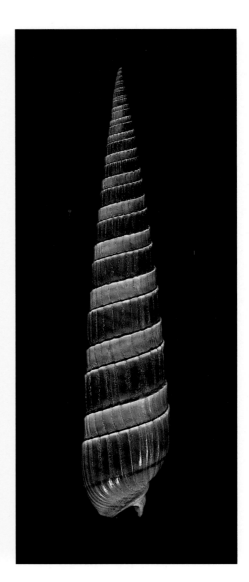

Terebridae
Terebra subulata
Distribution: Indo-Pacific
Average size: 4.3 inches (11 cm)
Frequency: Moderately common

Terebridae
Terebra triseriata
Distribution: Southwest Pacific Ocean
Average size: 4 inches (10 cm)
Frequency: Uncommon
Observations: Large specimens can have up
to 50 spiral turns.

Turritellidae
Turritella terebra
Distribution: Southwest Pacific Ocean
Average size: 5.5 inches (14 cm)
Frequency: Locally abundant
Observations: Found at low tide in the sand
and mud

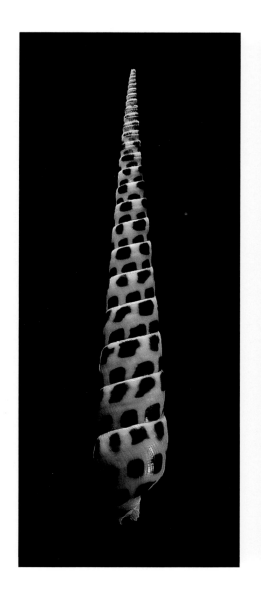
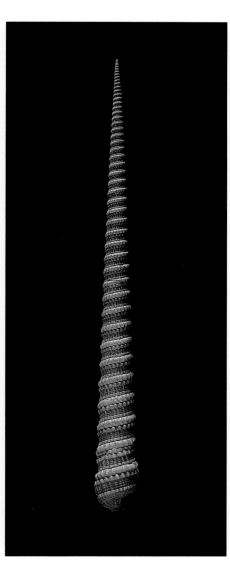
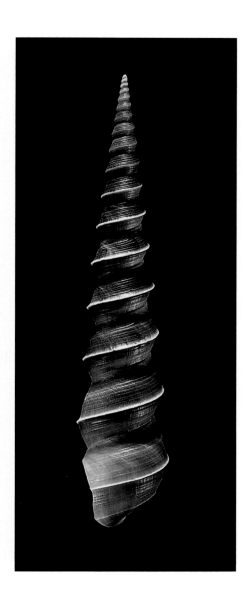

Tonnidae

Tonna tesselata

Distribution: South Africa and western
Pacific Ocean

Average size: 4 inches (10 cm)

Frequency: Common

Observations: Several synonyms, including
Dolium fimbriatum and *Dolium minjac*

Calliostomatidae
Calliostoma annulatum
Distribution: From Alaska to Southern
California, widely distributed from 3–65 feet
(1–20 m)
Average size: 1 inch (2.5 cm)
Frequency: Common

▶

Calliostomatidae

Calliostoma canaliculata

Distribution: From Alaska to California, widely distributed on floating algae

Average size: 1.2 inches (3 cm)

Frequency: Common

▼

Calliostomatidae

Calliostoma formosense

Distribution: Japan to Taiwan

Average size: 2 inches (5 cm)

Frequency: Common in deep water to depths of 1,000 feet (300 m)

Observations: The most impressive of all *Calliostoma*

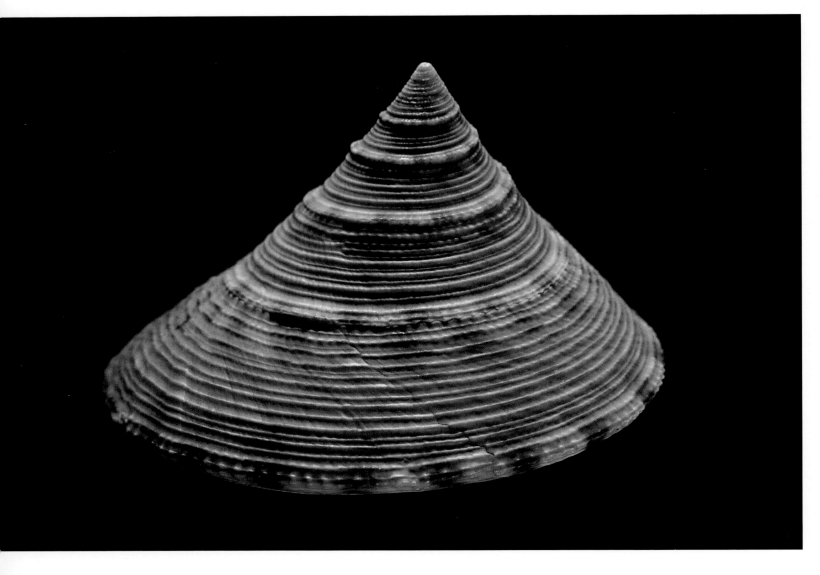

Calliostomatidae
Calliostoma foveauxana
Distribution: New Zealand
Average size: 0.6 inch (1.5 cm)
Frequency: Relatively rare

Trochidae

Bathybembix crumpii

Distribution: Sea of Japan

Average size: 1 inch (2.5 cm)

Frequency: Uncommon

Observations: Dredged on muddy soil at
650–1,000 feet (200–300 m); in some
species the nacre is almost entirely visible.

Trochidae

Trochus glyptus »

Distribution: New South Wales, Australia

Average size: 0.8 inch (2 cm)

Frequency: Rare

Observations: Dredged to 800 feet (240 m)

Trochidae

Clanculus pharaonius »

Distribution: Indian Ocean, under rocks in
the intertidal zone

Average size: 0.8 inch (2 cm)

Frequency: Locally common

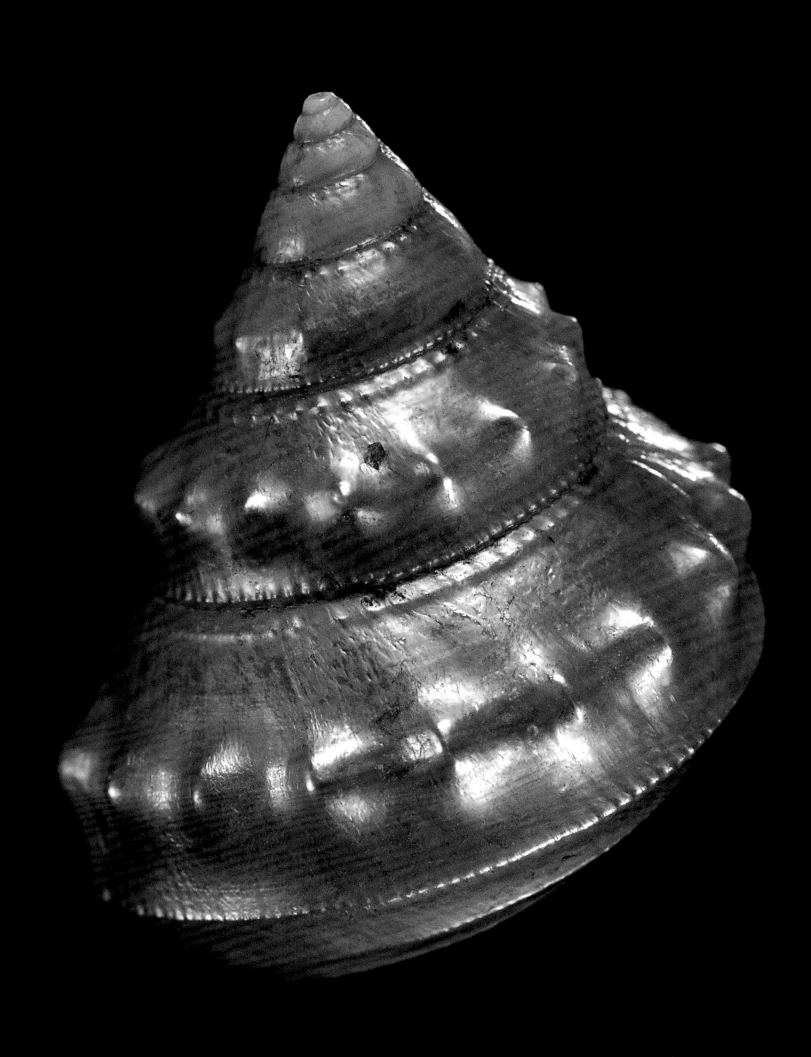

Trochidae
Trochus dentatus
Distribution: Red Sea and Europe
(the Adriatic)
Average size: 2 inches (5 cm)
Frequency: Moderately rare in the Adriatic
Observations: Found on reefs at
low tide

Turbinellidae
Altivasum flindersi (Vasum flindersi)
Distribution: South and west Australia,
widely distributed in deep water
Average size: 5.9 inches (15 cm)
Frequency: Uncommon

▶

Turbinellidae
Columbarium juliae
Distribution: East Africa, Mozambique
Average size: 3.1 inches (8 cm)
Frequency: Rare
Observations: Commonly called "pagoda shells," their elegant shape makes these specimens highly prized.

▼

Turbinellidae
Columbarium spinicinctum
Distribution: Eastern Australia
Average size: 2 inches (5 cm)
Frequency: Uncommon

Turbinellidae
Columbarium pagoda
Distribution: Widely in Japan and Thailand
Average size: 2 inches (5 cm)
Frequency: Common

Turbinellidae
Columbarium formosissimum
Distribution: Widely in South Africa
Average size: 2 inches (5 cm)
Frequency: Uncommon
Observations: Dredged to 650 feet (200 m)

Turbinellidae
Columbarium eastwoodae
Distribution: South Africa, Mozambique
Average size: 2.6 inches (6.5 cm)
Frequency: Relatively rare

Turbinellidae
Columbarium eastwoodae
Distribution: South Africa, Mozambique
Average size: 2.6 inches (6.5 cm)
Frequency: Relatively rare

Turbinellidae
Columbarium brayi
Distribution: The Caribbean
Average size: 2 inches (5 cm)
Frequency: Rare
Observations: Dredged to
1,000 feet (300 m)

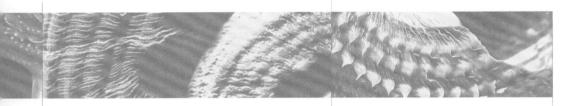

Turbinidae
Angaria delphinus
Distribution: Widely in the Philippines,
in nets
Average size: 2.4 inches (6 cm)
— including spines
Frequency: Uncommon
Observations: Synonymous with
Angaria imperialis Reeve

Turbinidae
Angaria vicdani
Distribution: To the south of the Philippines,
widely distributed in deep water
Average size: 1.8 inches (4.5 cm)
Frequency: Uncommon

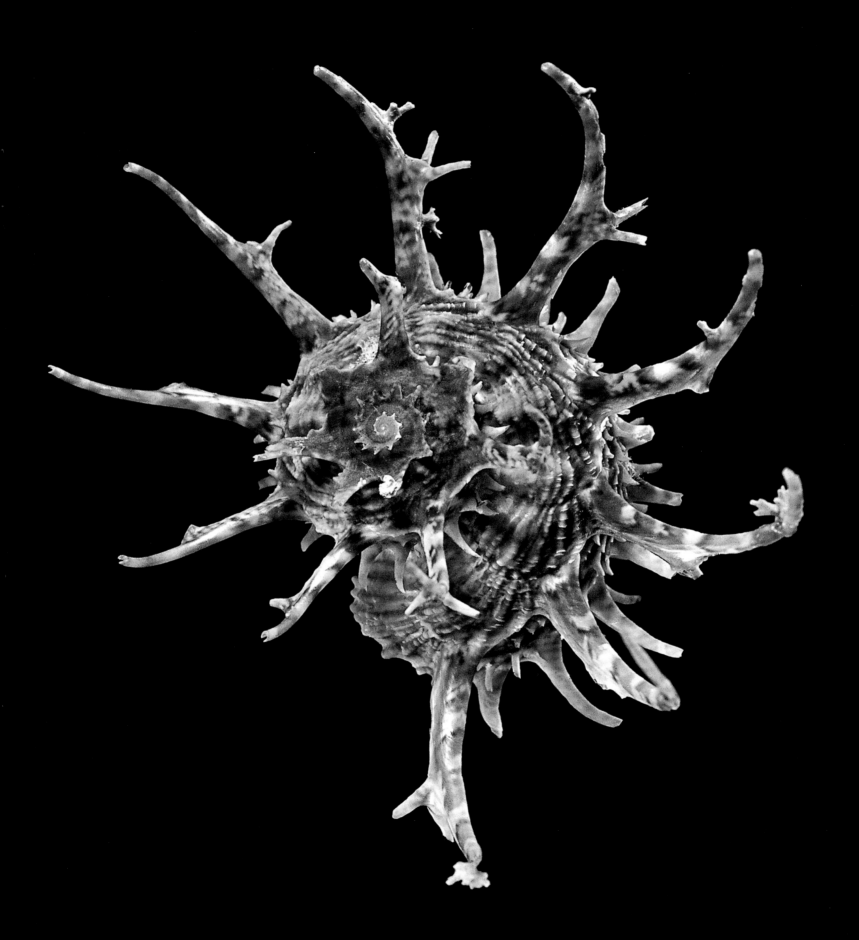

Turbinidae
Angaria delphinus
Distribution: Widely in the Philippines,
in nets
Average size: 2.4 inches (6 cm)
— including spines
Frequency: Uncommon
Observations: Synonymous with *Angaria*
imperialis Reeve

Turbinidae
Bolma girgyllus
Distribution: The Philippines and Taiwan, in deep water
Average size: 2 inches (5 cm)
Frequency: Rare

Turbinidae
Bolma girgyllus
Distribution: The Philippines and Taiwan, in deep water
Average size: 2 inches (5 cm)
Frequency: Rare

Turbinidae
Bolma girgyllus
Distribution: The Philippines and Taiwan, in
deep water
Average size: 2 inches (5 cm)
Frequency: Rare

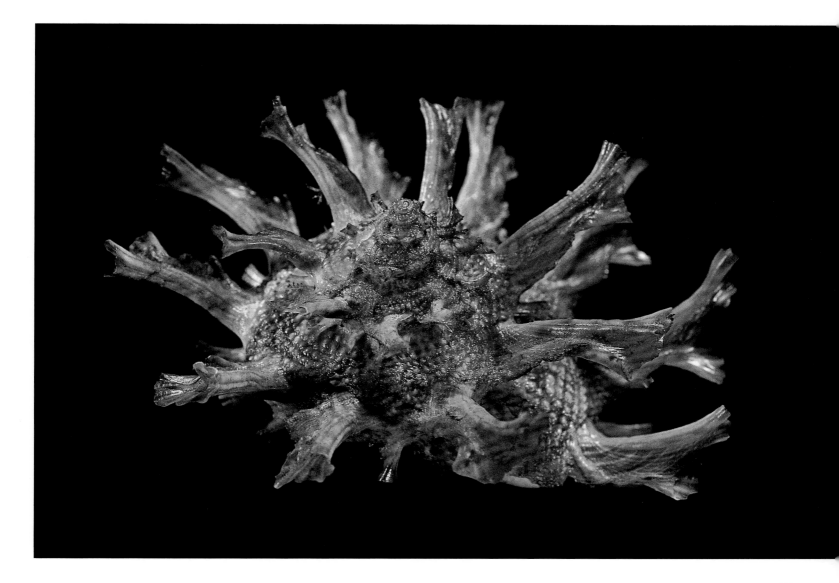

Turbinidae

Astraea heliotropium

Distribution: New Zealand, widely
distributed in deep water

Average size: 3.1 inches (8 cm)

Frequency: Uncommon

Observations: Synonymous with *Angaria
imperialis* Gmelin

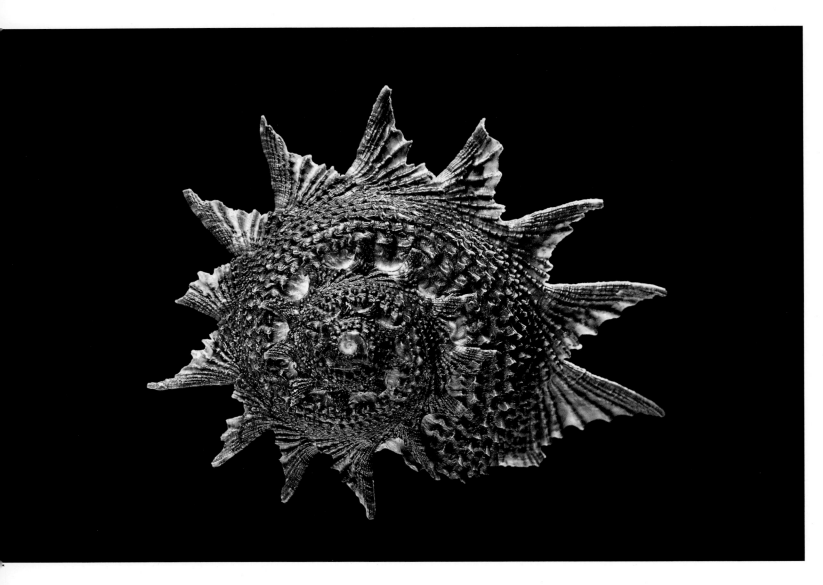

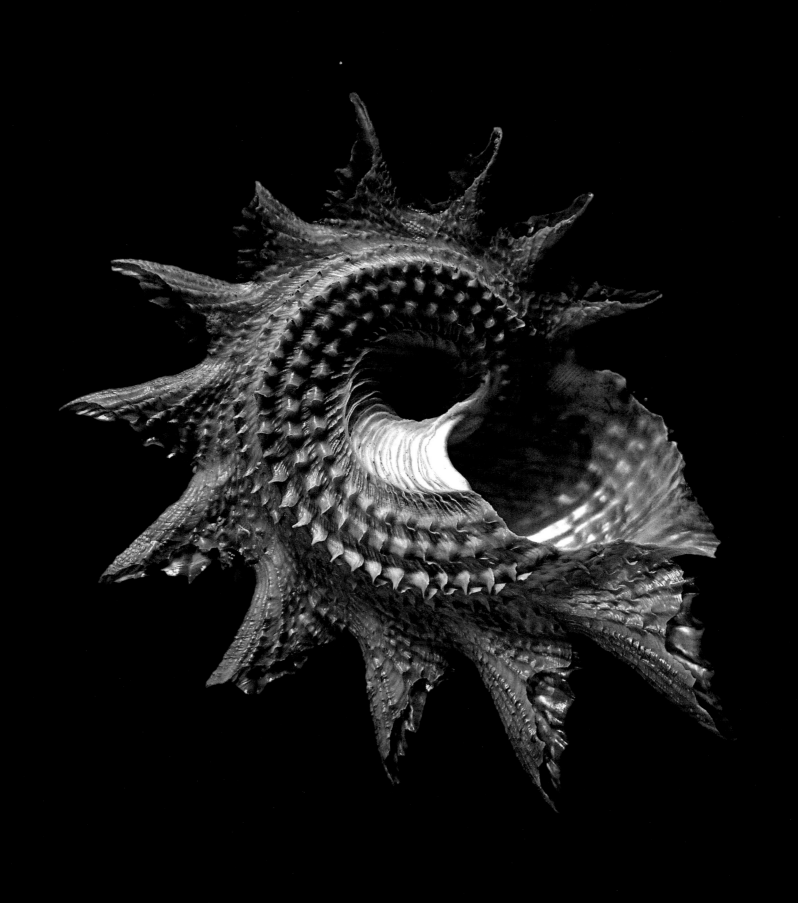

Turbinidae
Guildfordia yoka
Distribution: Japan, widely distributed
in deep water
Average size: 2.8 inches (7 cm)
— including spines
Frequency: Relatively common

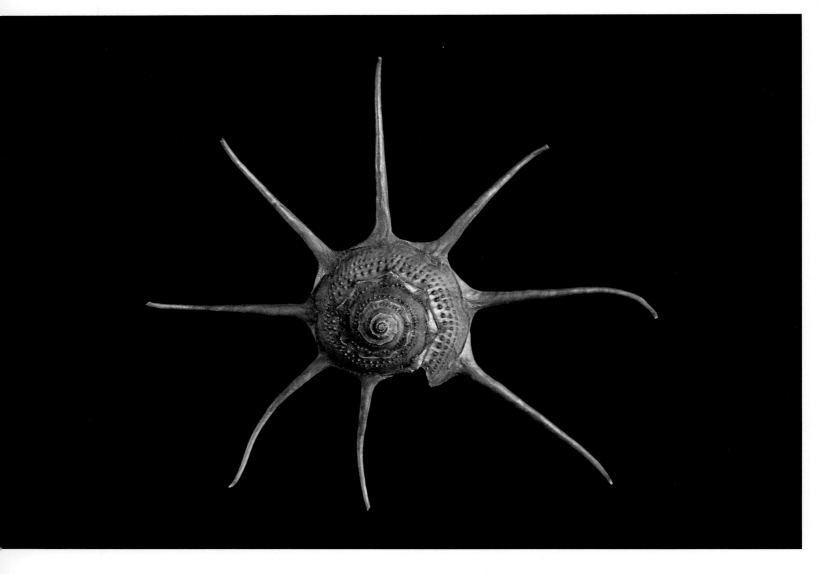

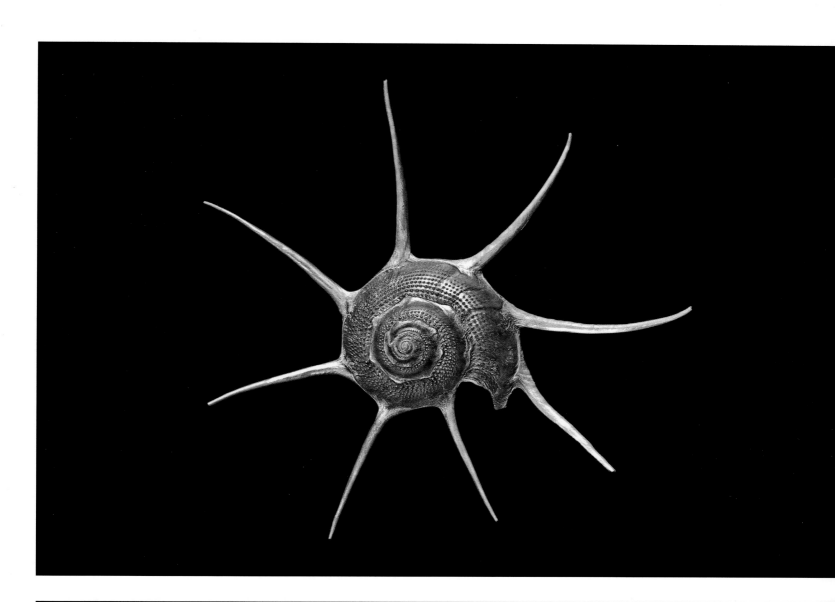

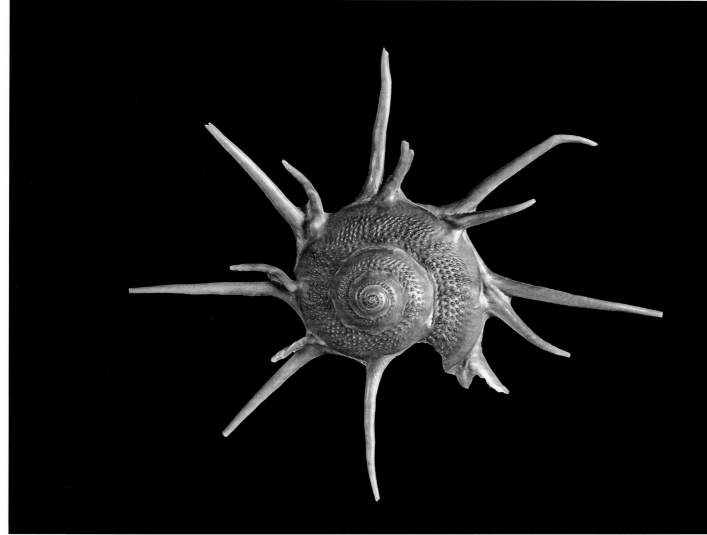

Turbinidae

Turbo argyrostomus

Distribution: Indo-Pacific

Average size: 2.4 inches (6 cm)

Frequency: Common on reefs

Observations: One variety has long spines.

Turbinidae

Turbo torquatus

Distribution: Southern Australia

Average size: 2 inches (5 cm)

Frequency: Uncommon

Observations: Dredged to 80 feet (25 m)

Turbinidae

Turbo petholatus ➳

Distribution: Central and western Pacific
Ocean, in shallow water

Average size: 2 inches (5 cm)

Frequency: Common on reefs

Observations: Its beautiful operculum, called
"cat's eye," is used in jewelry.

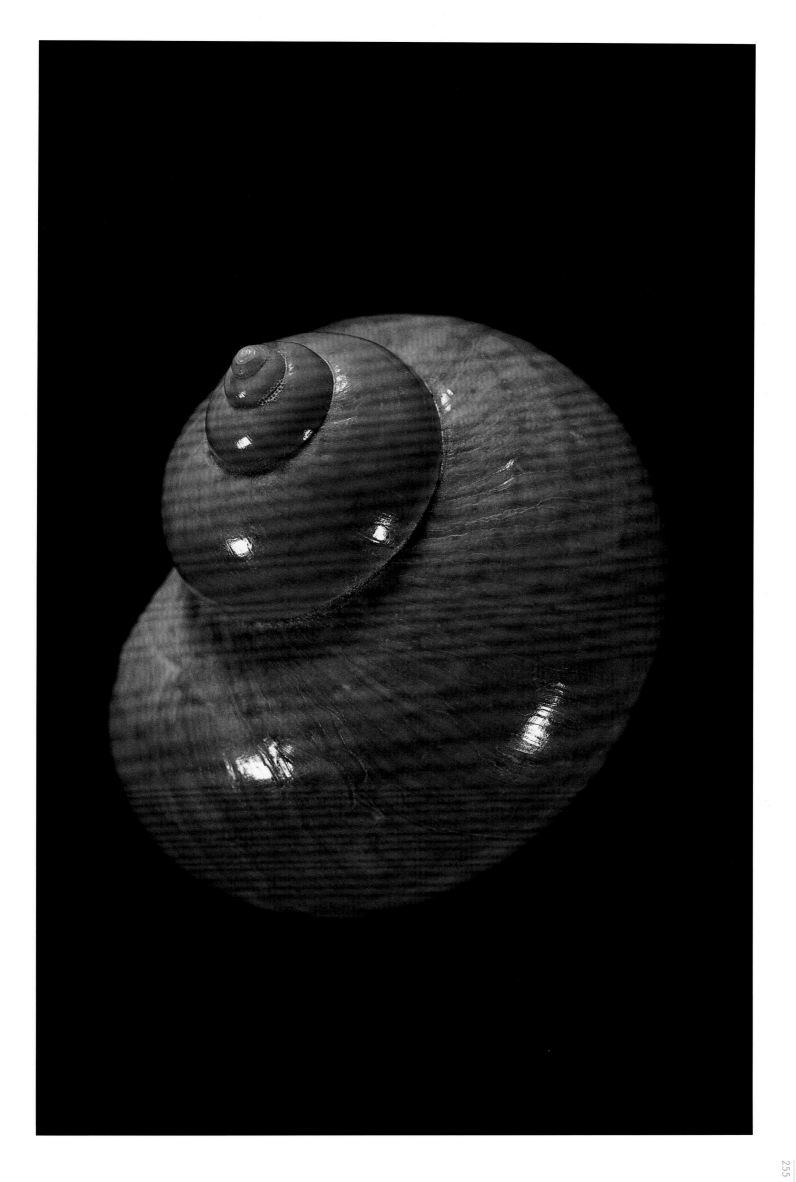

Turridae
Thatcheria mirabilis
Distribution: Japan to the Philippines,
in deep water
Average size: 3.1 inches (8 cm)
Frequency: Common
Observations: Some authors place it in
its own family: Thatcheriidae.

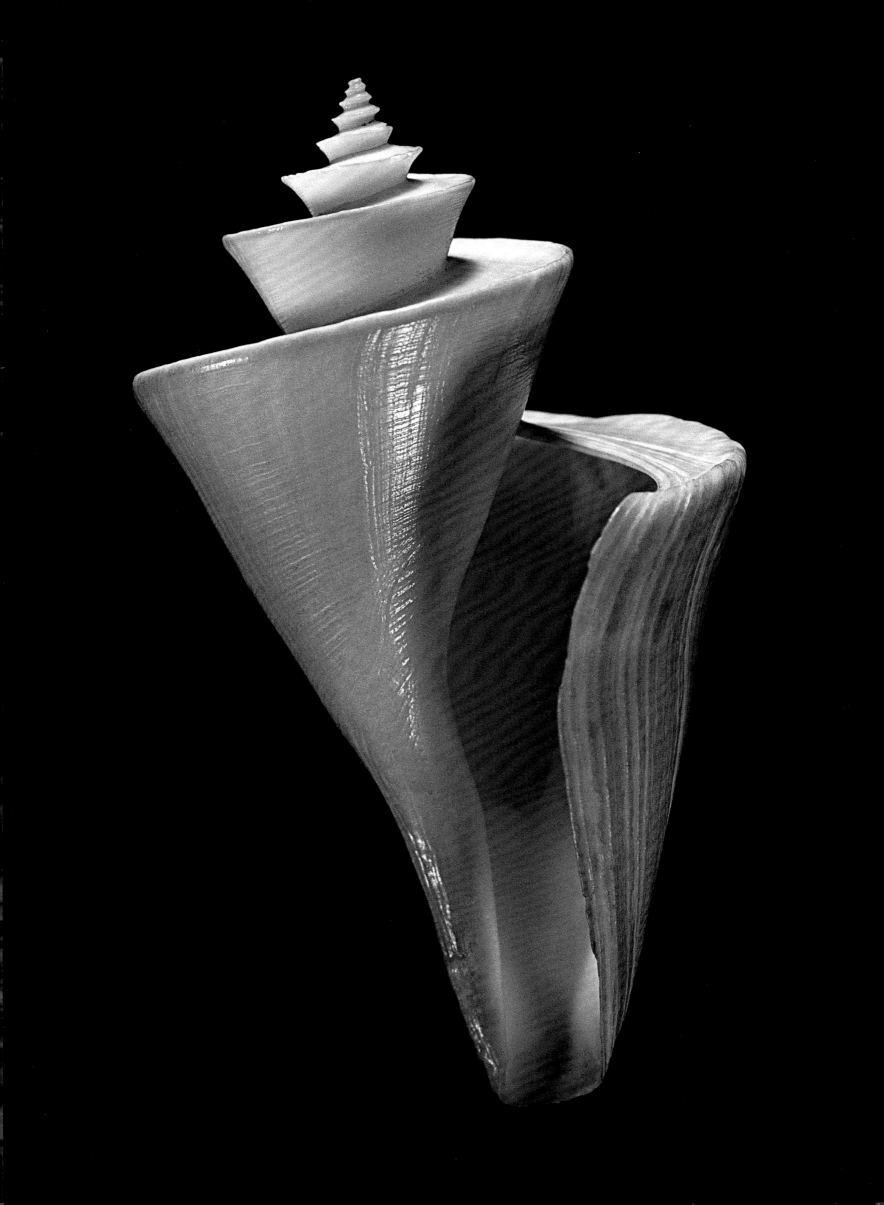

Turridae
Nihonia australis
Distribution: Western Pacific Ocean
Average size: 2.4 inches (6 cm)
Frequency: Rare
Observations: Dredged to 260–330 feet
(80–100 m)

Turridae
Gemmula cosmoi
Distribution: East Africa, Mozambique
Average size: 2 inches (5 cm)
Frequency: Locally common

Turridae
Fusiturricula jaquensis
Distribution: Columbia
Average size: 2.4 inches (6 cm)
Frequency: Uncommon
Observations: Trawled at about 130 feet
(40 m)

Turridae

Tiariturris spectabilis

Distribution: Indo-Pacific, under coral

Average size: 2 inches (5 cm)

Frequency: Uncommon

Turridae

Lophiotoma polytropa

Distribution: The Philippines, Maluku Islands and New Caledonia

Average size: 1.2 inches (4 cm)

Frequency: Uncommon

Turridae

Lophiotoma indica

Distribution: Sri Lanka to Australia and Fiji, in moderately deep water

Average size: 3.1 inches (8 cm)

Frequency: Uncommon

Turridae
Bathytoma lühdorfi
Distribution: The Philippines
Average size: 1.2 inches (4 cm)
Frequency: Relatively common
Observations: Caught with tangle nets

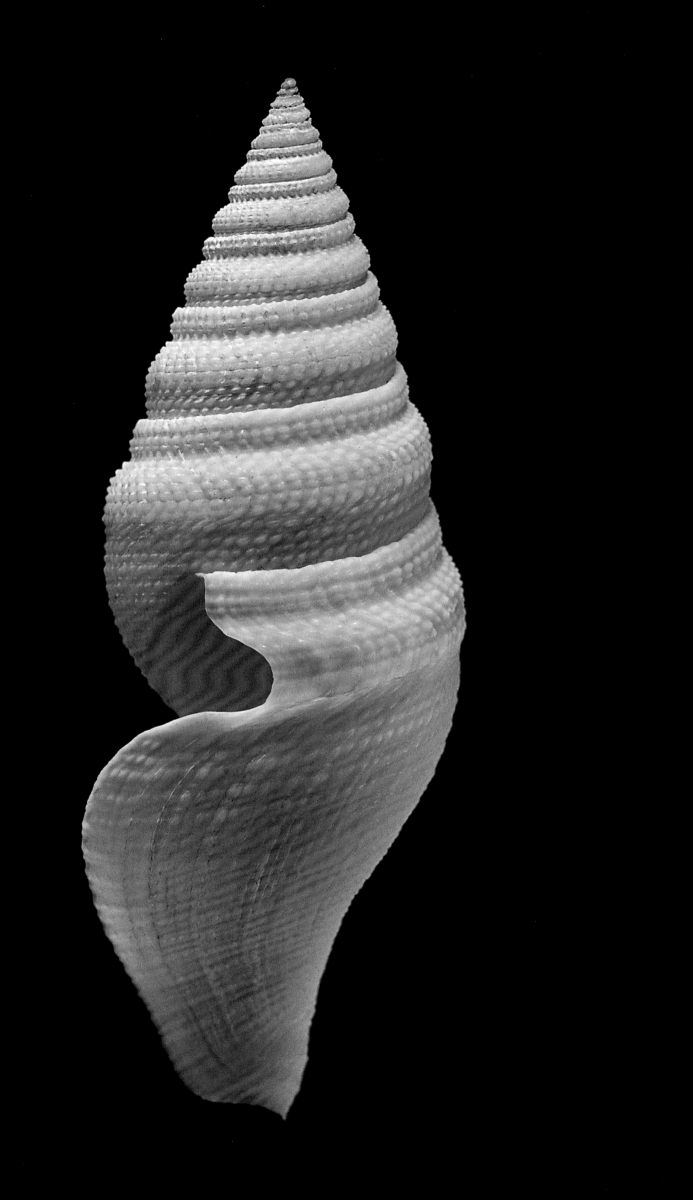

Volutidae
Livonia roadnightae
Distribution: Southern Australia
Average size: 7 inches (18 cm)
Frequency: Uncommon
Observations: Dredged from 165–650 feet
(50–200 m)

►

Volutidae

Volutoconus bednalli

Distribution: Northern Territory, Australia,
on sand from depths of 32–131 feet
(10–40 m)
Average size: 4 inches (10 cm)
Frequency: Rare

Volutidae

Fulgoraria rupestris

Distribution: Taiwan and China
Average size: 4 inches (10 cm)
Frequency: Rare
Observations: Synonymous with
Fulgoraria aurantia

▼

Volutidae

Paramoria guntheri

Distribution: Southern Australia
Average size: 1.2 inches (4 cm)
Frequency: Moderately rare
Observations: Exemplary specimens
are rare.

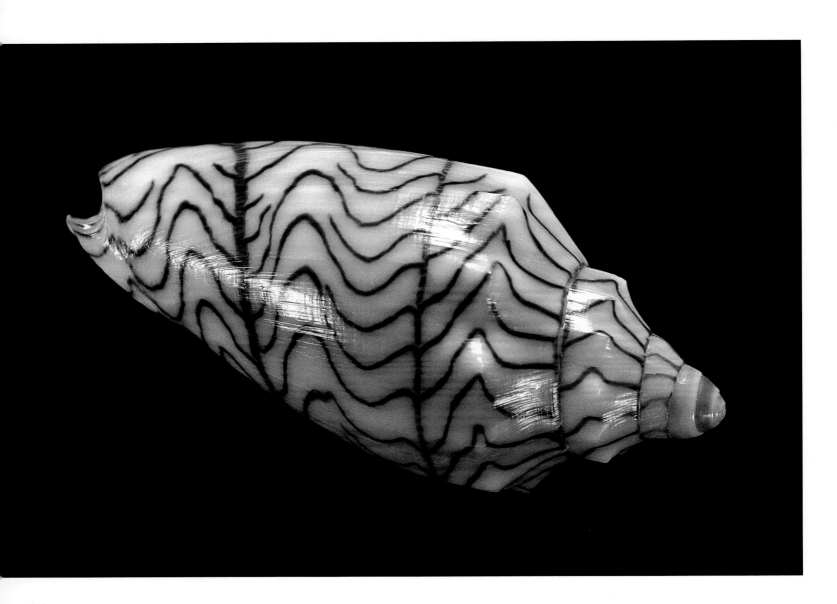

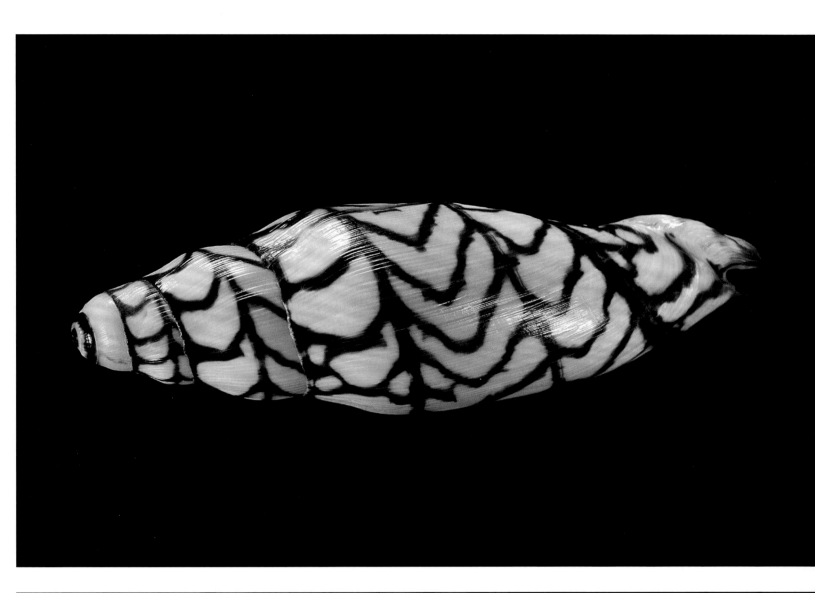

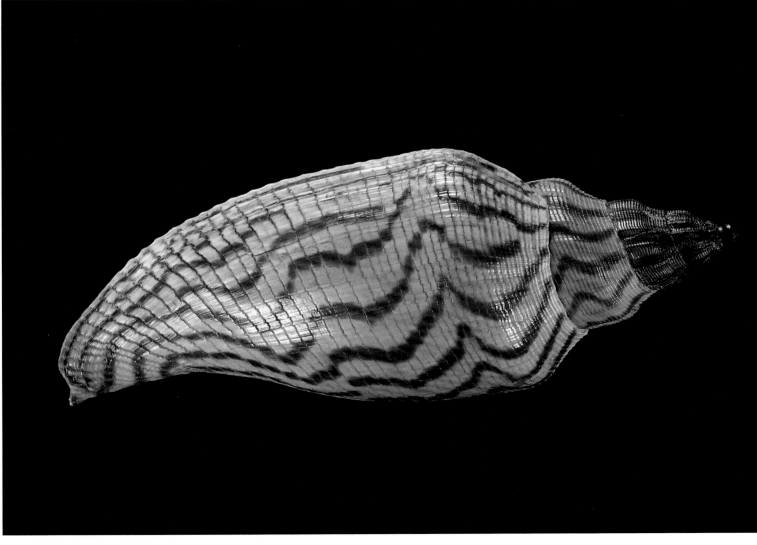

▶

Volutidae

Lyria kurodai

Distribution: Endemic to Taiwan

Average size: 3.1 inches (8 cm)

Frequency: Rare

Observations: Dredged to 145 feet (44 m)

Volutidae

Lyria lyraeformis

Distribution: Eastern Africa, in medium-depth water

Average size: 4 inches (10 cm)

Frequency: Uncommon

▼

Volutidae

Calliotectum johnsoni dupreyi

Distribution: Southwest Pacific Ocean, in deep water

Average size: 4 inches (10 cm)

Frequency: Uncommon

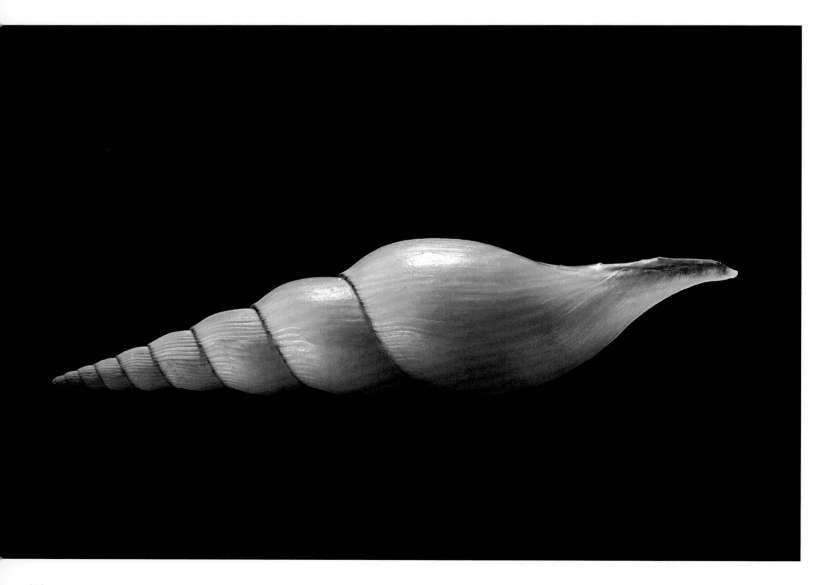

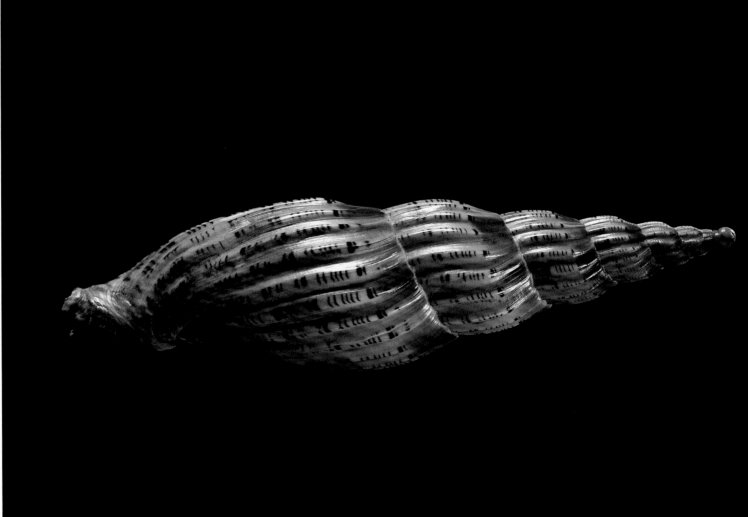

Volutidae

Voluta georginae

Distribution: Queensland, Western Australia
and the Philippines

Average size: 6 inches (15 cm)

Frequency: Rare in the Philippines

Observations: Trawled at great depths

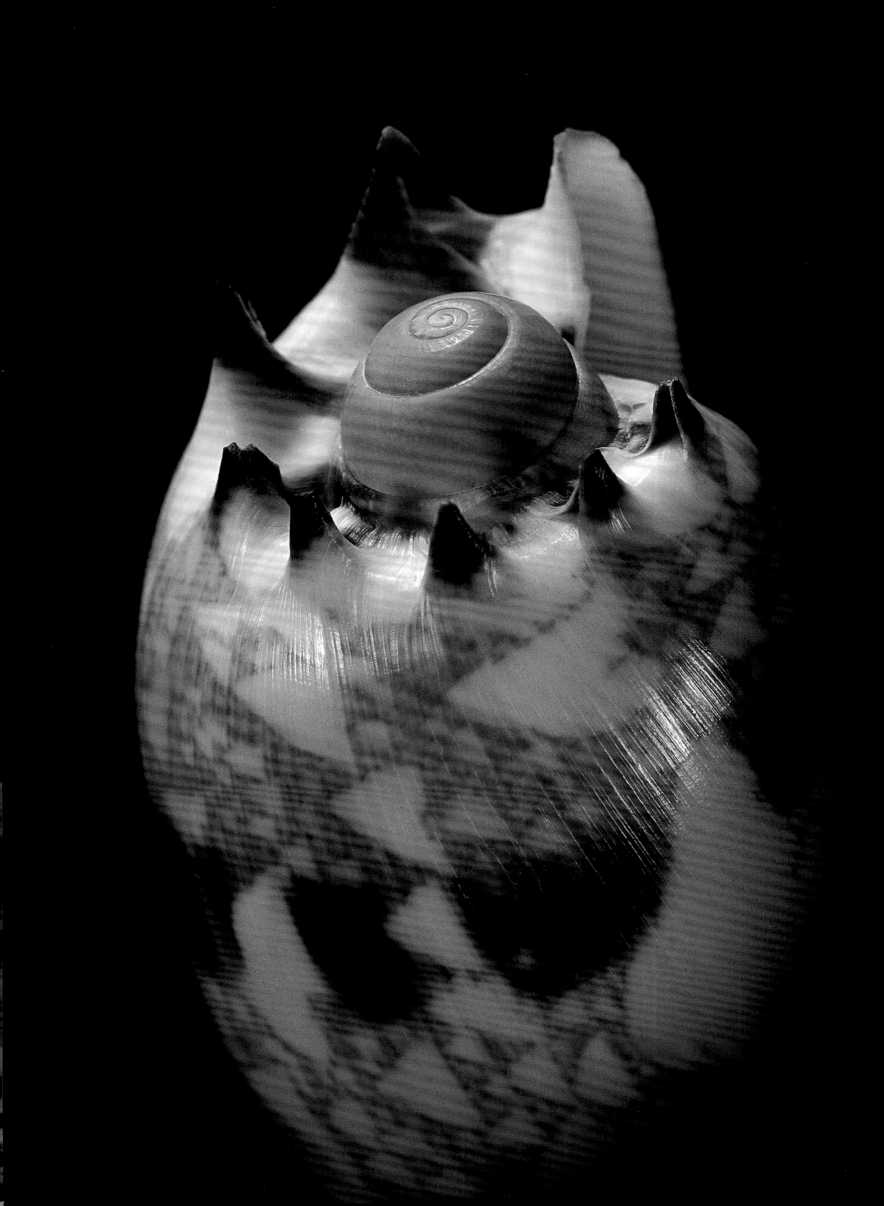

Volutidae
Cymbiola aulica cathcartiae
Distribution: Southern Philippines
Average size: 3.5 inches (9 cm)
Frequency: Uncommon
Observations: Shows variation in its nodes
and the absence of the red coloration of
Cymbiola aulica

Volutidae
Cymbiola aulica cathcartiae
Distribution: Southern Philippines
Average size: 3.5 inches (9 cm)
Frequency: Uncommon
Observations: Shows variation in its nodes
and the absence of the red coloration of
Cymbiola aulica

Volutidae

Melo melo

Distribution: Malaysia and the South China
Sea, on muddy soil to 30 feet (10 m)
Average size: 7.9 inches (20 cm)
Frequency: Uncommon

Volutidae

Melo melo

Distribution: Malaysia and the South China
Sea, on muddy soil to 30 feet (10 m)
Average size: 7.9 inches (20 cm)
Frequency: Uncommon

Volutidae
Melo broderipii
Distribution: The Philippines
Average size: Up to 12 inches
(30 cm)
Frequency: Rare

▼

Volutidae
Aulica imperialis
Distribution: The Philippines, on sand in
shallow water
Average size: 8 inches (20 cm)
Frequency: Common

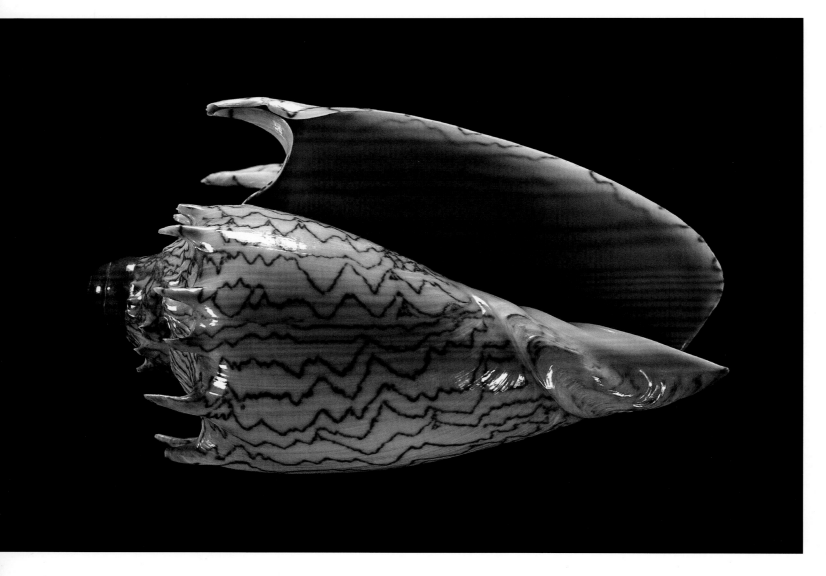

Volutidae
Melo broderipii
Distribution: The Philippines
Average size: Up to 12 inches
(30 cm)
Frequency: Rare

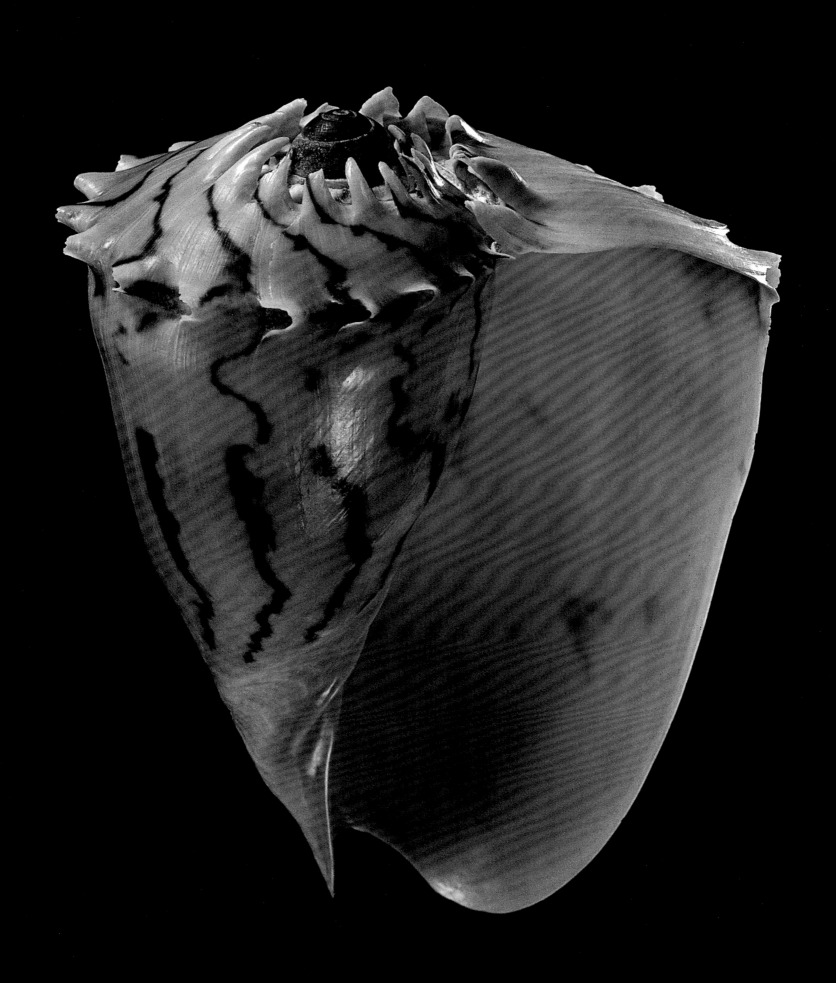

Volutidae
Fulgoraria (Psephaea) concinna corrugata
Distribution: Kii Channel, Japan
Average size: Varies from
3.5–7.1 inches (9–18 cm)
Frequency: Common
Observations: This subspecies
is distinguished by its color variations.

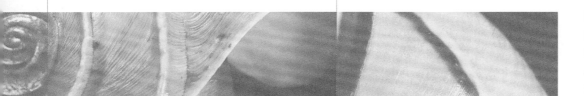

Bradybaenidae
Chloraea sirena
Distribution: The Philippine archipelago
Average size: 1 inch (2.5 cm)
Frequency: Uncommon

Bradybaenidae
Calocochlia (Pyrochilus) pyrostoma
Distribution: Indonesia, Halmera and
Maluku Islands
Average size: 2.4 inches (6 cm)
Frequency: Rare

Ariophantidae
Asperitas polymorpha
Distribution: Indonesia
Average size: 1 inch (2.5 cm)
Frequency: Fairly rare
Observations: Extremely variable colors

Ariophantidae
Elaphroconcha cochlostyloides
Distribution: Indonesia, in equatorial
forests/rain forests
Average size: 1.2 inches (3 cm)
Frequency: Relatively common

Camaenidae

Amphidromus floresianus

Distribution: South of Flores and Sumbawa in Indonesia

Average size: 1.4 inches (3.5 cm)

Frequency: Locally common

Observations: Fifty percent of the individuals in this species are sinistral (coiling clockwise).

▶

Camaenidae
Amphidromus perversus
Distribution: Indonesia from east Sumatra to Bali
Average size: 1.6 inches (4 cm)
Frequency: Locally common
Observations: At least ten names have been given to distinguish between a variety of colors.

▼

Camaenidae
Papuina pulcherrima
Distribution: Papua New Guinea, Manus Island
Average size: 1.4 inches (3.5 cm)
Frequency: Common, but it is considered an endangered species
Observations: The green color of the shell changes to brown after the rainy season ends.

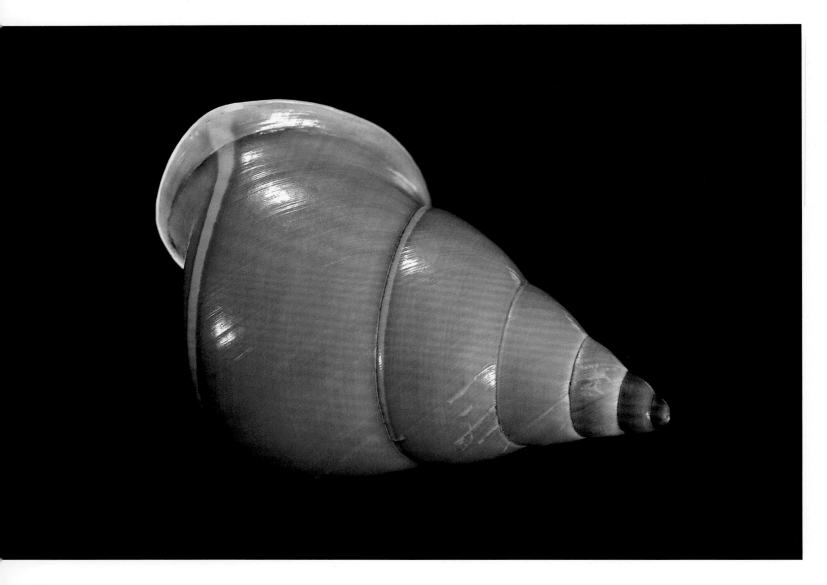

Cyclophoridae
Rhiostoma housei
Distribution: Thailand, Ko Samui and Gulf of Siam
Average size: 1 inch (2.5 cm)
Frequency: Locally common
Observations: A narrow channel connects the opening to a siphon to allow breathing during periods of low water levels (similar to a snorkel).

Helminthoglyptidae
Polymita picta
Distribution: Eastern Cuba
Average size: 1 inch (2.5 cm)
Frequency: Becoming rarer due to the
destructive effect of insecticides
Observations: The most beautiful and
most desired of all terrestrial mollusks

Odontostomidae

Anostoma octodentatus depressum

Distribution: Brazil

Average size: 1 inch (2.5 cm)

Frequency: Rare

Observations: The opening is protected
by several "teeth."

Orthalicidae
Bostryx weyrauchi
Distribution: Peru (Ninabamba and
Ayacucho regions)
Average size: 0.8 inch (2 cm)
Frequency: Locally rare
Observations: The genus *Bostryx* consists
of species totally different from one
another in both shape and color.

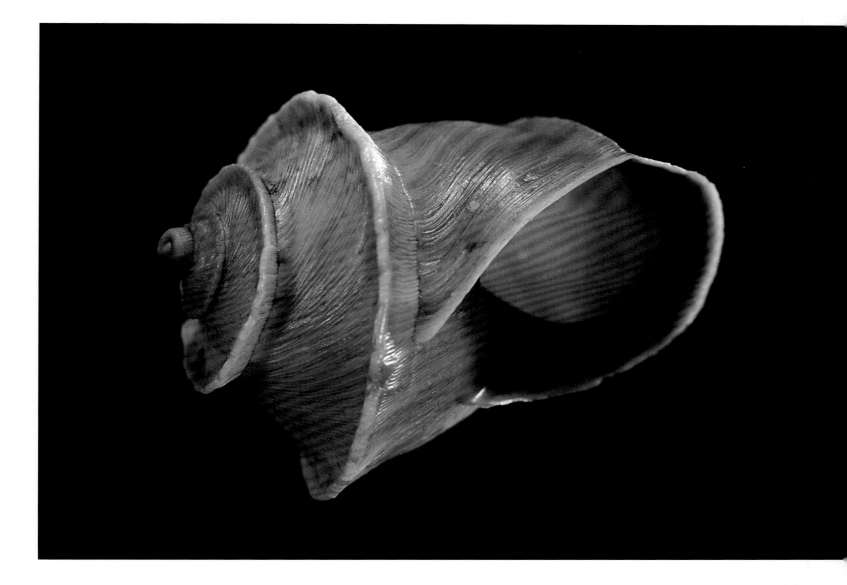

Orthalicidae
Bostryx weyrauchi
Distribution: Peru (Ninabamba and
Ayacucho regions)
Average size: 0.8 inch (2 cm)
Frequency: Locally rare

Orthalicidae
Liguus virgineus
Distribution: Cuba, Santo Domingo
and Haiti
Average size: 1.8 inches (4.5 cm)
Frequency: From abundant to uncommon
Observations: Overharvested, the *Liguus*
are becoming rarer; it is estimated that
millions of these beautiful snails were sent
by boat to the United States in the 1980s.
There are 120 design and color forms of
this species.

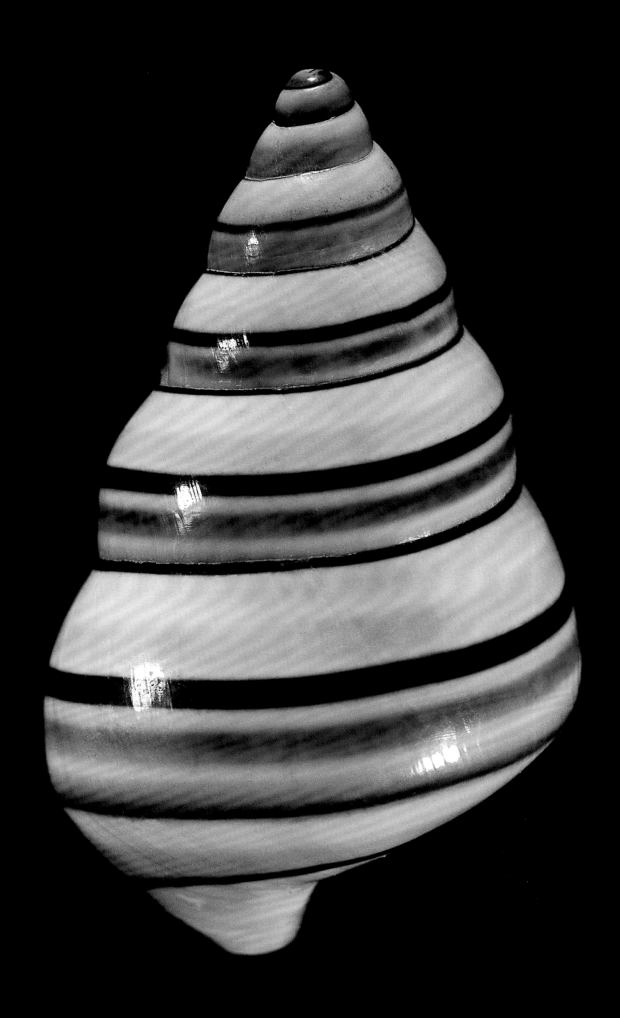

Pomatiasidae

Tropidophora cuveriana

Distribution: Northeast of Madagascar

Average size: 2.8 inches (7 cm)

Frequency: Extinct

Observations: Fortunately, there remain nearly 20 other species of *Tropidophora*, though only one, *Tropidophora deburghiae*, is as imposing as this one, which is typical of the genus.

Cardiidae
Trachycardium quadragenarium
Distribution: California to Mexico, in the
intertidal zone to depths of 400 feet
(120 m)
Average size: Up to 6 inches (15 cm)
Frequency: Common

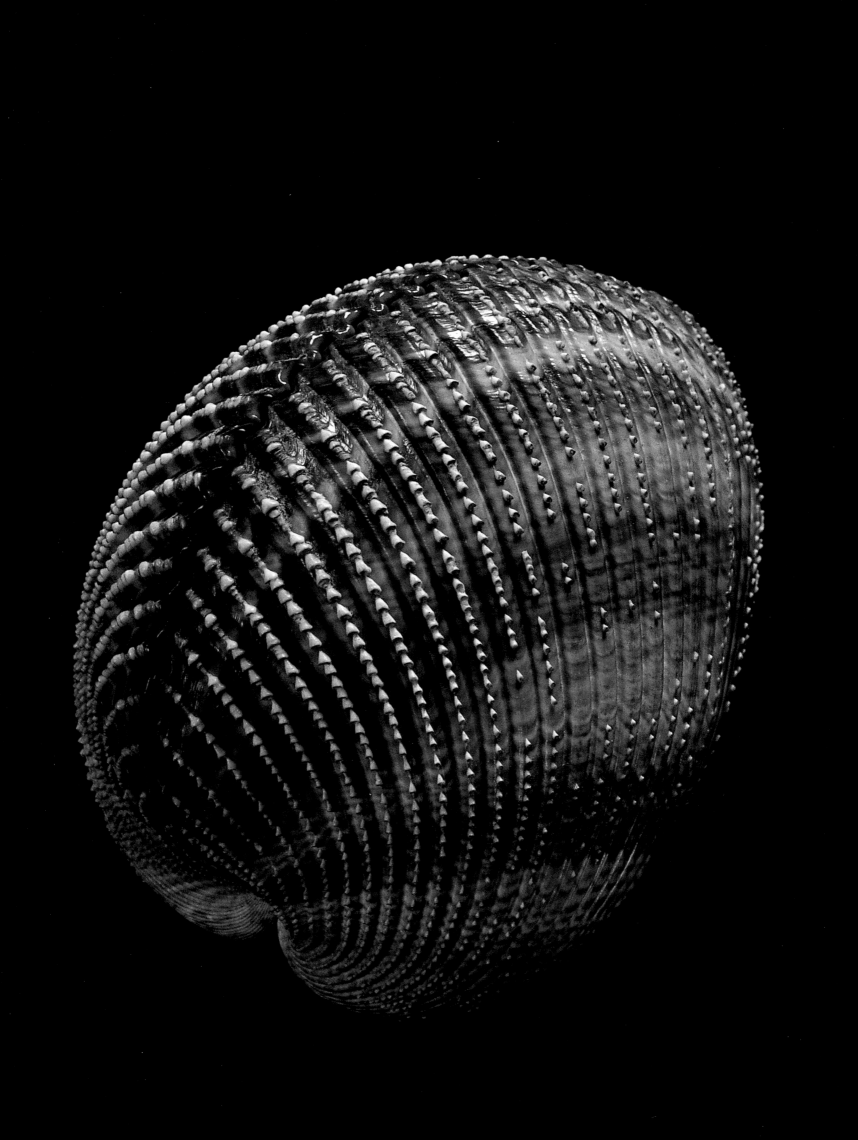

Cardiidae

Ctenocardia victor

Distribution: Western Pacific Ocean, widely distributed to depths of 325 feet (100 m)

Average size: 1 inch (2.5 cm)

Frequency: Uncommon

Cardiidae

Ctenocardia victor

Distribution: Western Pacific Ocean, widely distributed to depths of 325 feet (100 m)

Average size: 1 inch (2.5 cm)

Frequency: Uncommon

Nemocardium bechei

Distribution: From Australia to Japan, widely
distributed from 30–200 feet (10–70 m)
Average size: 2 inches (5 cm)
Frequency: Moderately common

Cardiidae
Nemocardium bechei
Distribution: From Australia to Japan, widely
distributed from 30–200 feet (10–70 m)
Average size: 2 inches (5 cm)
Frequency: Moderately common

Cardiidae

Frigidocardium exasperatum

Distribution: Queensland, Western Australia,
in shallow water
Average size: 1.2 inches (4 cm)
Frequency: Uncommon

Cardiidae

Corculum cardissa ⇥

Distribution: The Indo-Pacific, in the sand
at average depths
Average size: 2 inches (5 cm)
Frequency: Locally common

Glossidae
Meiocardia moltkiana
Distribution: Eastern India, in shallow water
Average size: 1.2 inches (3 cm)
Frequency: Uncommon

Pectinidae
Chlamys islandicus
Distribution: Western Atlantic from the
Arctic to Massachusetts and down to
Washington, D.C., northern Europe
Average size: 2.8 inches (7 cm)
Frequency: Abundant

Pectinidae
Gloripallium pallium
Distribution: Indo-Pacific
Average size: 2.4 inches (6 cm)
Frequency: Locally common

Pectinidae
Pecten flabellum
Distribution: West Africa from Mauritania
to Angola in shallow water
Average size: 2 inches (5 cm)
Frequency: Moderately common

▼
Pectinidae
Gloripallium speciosum
Distribution: The Philippines
and Japan
Average size: 1.2 inches (4 cm)
Frequency: Locally common

Pectinidae
Chlamys imbricata
Distribution: The Caribbean, Bahamas
and Florida
Average size: 2 inches (5 cm)
Frequency: Uncommon

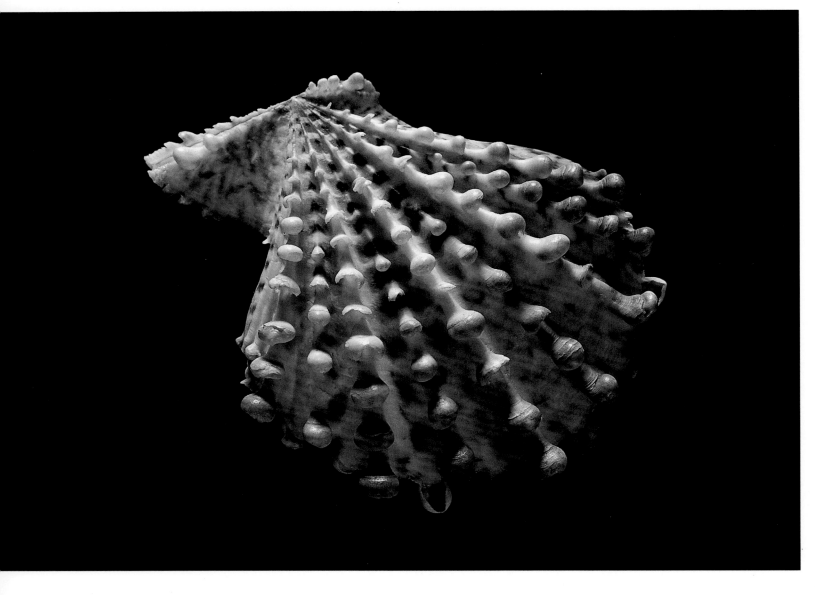

Pectinidae
Chlamys imbricata
Distribution: The Caribbean, Bahamas
and Florida
Average size: 2 inches (5 cm)
Frequency: Uncommon

Pectinidae

Mirapecten mirificus

Distribution: From the Philippines
to Hawaii, to depths of 650 feet
(200 m)

Average size: 1.2 inches (4 cm)

Frequency: Uncommon

Pectinidae
Chlamys rastellum
Distribution: The Indo-Pacific and the
Red Sea
Average size: 1.6 inches (4 cm)
Frequency: Uncommon
Observations: Red Sea specimens are
highly prized.

Pectinidae
Chlamys islandicus
Distribution: Western Atlantic from the
Arctic to Massachusetts and down to
Washington, D.C., northern Europe
Average size: 2.8 inches (7 cm)
Frequency: Abundant

Pectinidae
Equichlamys bifrons
Distribution: South Australia and Tasmania
Average size: 2.4 inches (6 cm)
Frequency: Uncommon

Pectinidae

Chlamys asperrima

Distribution: Australia and Tasmania, in the intertidal zone to depths of 325 feet (100 m)

Average size: 2.4 inches (6 cm)

Frequency: Uncommon

Pectinidae

Pecten ziczac

Distribution: Southeastern United States to
Brazil, from 3–130 feet (1–40 m)

Average size: 2.8 inches (7 cm)

Frequency: Locally common

Observations: The rare albino examples are
very sought after.

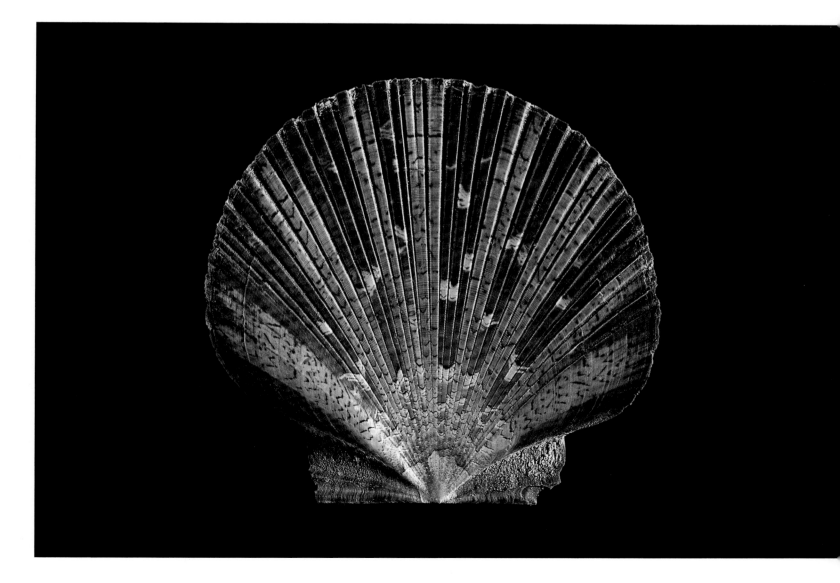

Pectinidae

Lyropecten nodosus

Distribution: From southeastern United States to Brazil, widely distributed to 100 feet (30 m)

Average size: 4 inches (10 cm)

Frequency: Locally common

Observations: Large examples with well-defined nodes are rare and therefore much sought after.

Pholadidae
Cyrtopleura costata
Distribution: East coast of the United
States to Brazil, in mud and small
amounts of water
Average size: 5.1 inches (13 cm)
Frequency: Locally common
Observations: Pink examples are
very rare.

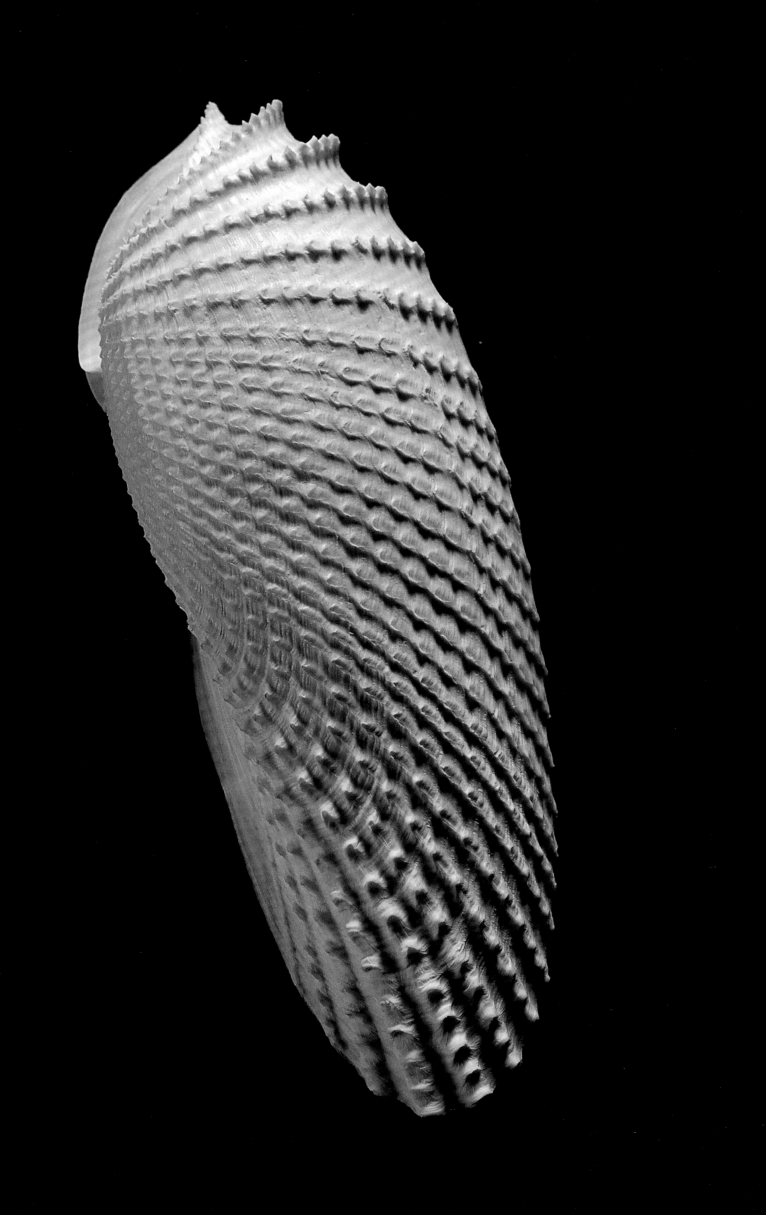

Spondylidae
Spondylus princeps
Distribution: From the Gulf of California
to Panama, widely distributed.
Average size: 4.7 inches (12 cm)
Frequency: Relatively rare

Spondylidae
Spondylus imbutus
Distribution: The Philippines
Average size: 1.2 inches (4 cm)
Frequency: Uncommon

Spondylidae
Spondylus regius
Distribution: Eastern Pacific Ocean, on
rocks, from depths of 15–30 feet (5–10 m)
Average size: 4 inches (10 cm)
Frequency: Common

Spondylidae
Spondylus americanus
Distribution: Western Atlantic from the
U.S. coast to Brazil, widely on shipwrecks
30–165 feet (9–50 m) deep
Average size: 4.7 inches (12 cm),
including spines
Frequency: Locally abundant

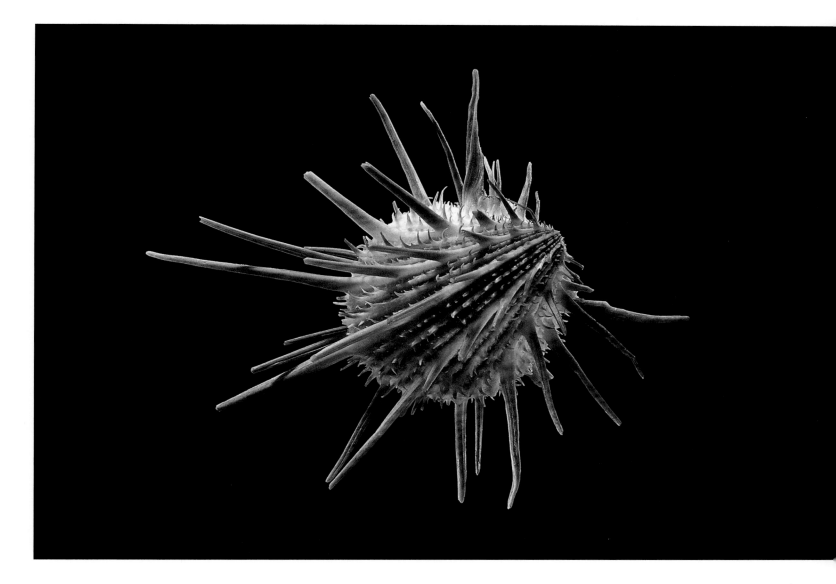

Spondylidae

Spondylus imperialis

Distribution: Japan, widely distributed
from 15–165 feet (5–50 m)

Average size: 2.8 inches (7 cm)

Frequency: Common

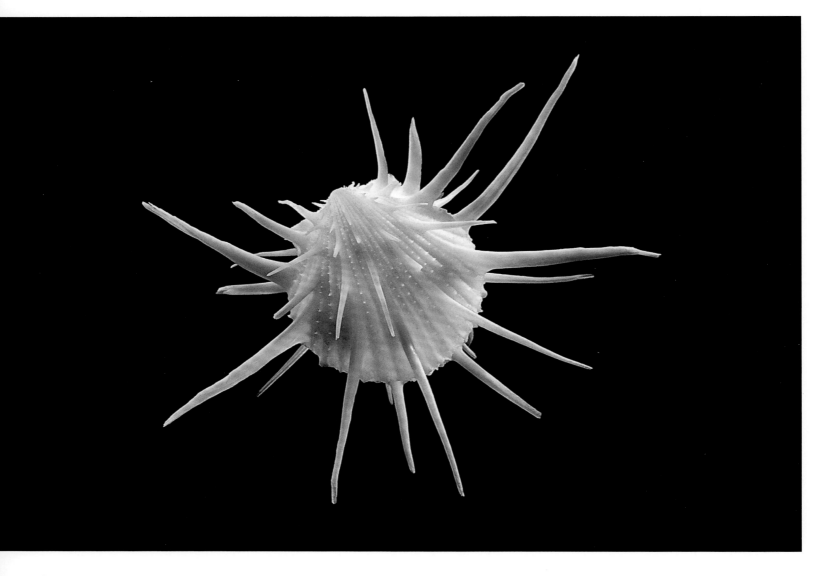

Spondylidae

Spondylus imperialis

Distribution: Japan, widely distributed
from 15–165 feet (5–50 m)

Average size: 2.8 inches (7 cm)

Frequency: Common

Spondylidae

Spondylus linguaefelis

Distribution: Hawaii and the Philippines

Average size: 3.1 inches (8 cm)

Frequency: Relatively rare

Observations: The beautiful examples found in the Hawaiian Islands are very sought after.

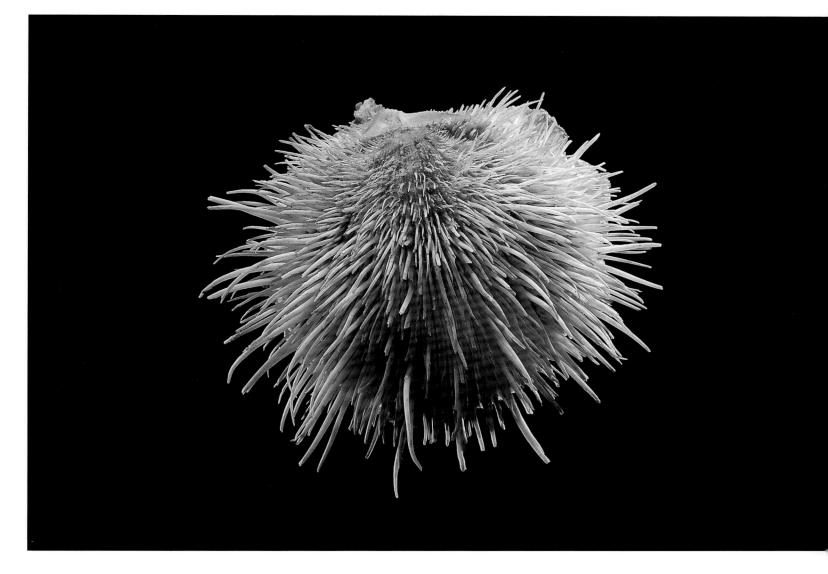

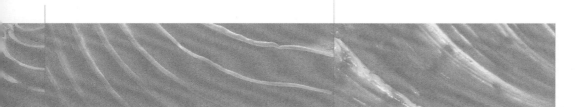

Tridacnidae
Hippopus hippopus
Distribution: Southwest Pacific, on coral
Average size: 8 inches (20 cm)
Frequency: Common

Tridacnidae
Hippopus hippopus
Distribution: Southwest Pacific, on coral
Average size: 8 inches (20 cm)
Frequency: Common

▶

Tridacnidae

Tridacna squamosa

Distribution: Indo-Pacific, with the exception
of Hawaii

Average size: 12 inches (30 cm)

Frequency: Locally common

Observations: In an effort to protect the
coral reefs they inhabit, it is illegal to
transport tridacnids onto American soil.

▼

Tridacnidae

Tridacna noae

Distribution: Indo-Pacific, on coral

Average size: 12 inches (30 cm)

Frequency: Once common, it is now rarer.

Observations: Synonymous with *Tridacna
squamosa*; it is a protected species.

Veneridae

Circomphalus foliaceolamellosa

Distribution: West Africa, in shallow water

Average size: 3.1 inches (8 cm)

Frequency: Locally common

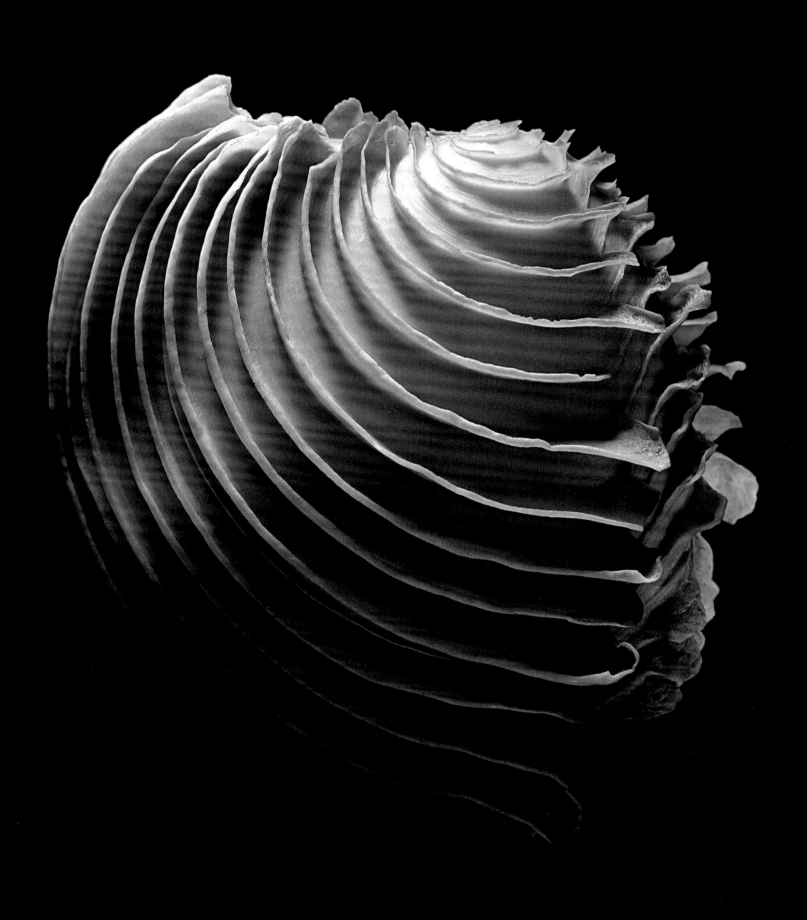

Veneridae

Callanaitis disjecta

Distribution: Southern Australia and
Tasmania to depths of 165 feet (50 m)

Average size: 2 inches (5 cm)

Frequency: Moderately common

Observations: Synonymous with
Callanaitis lemellata and *Bassina disjecta*

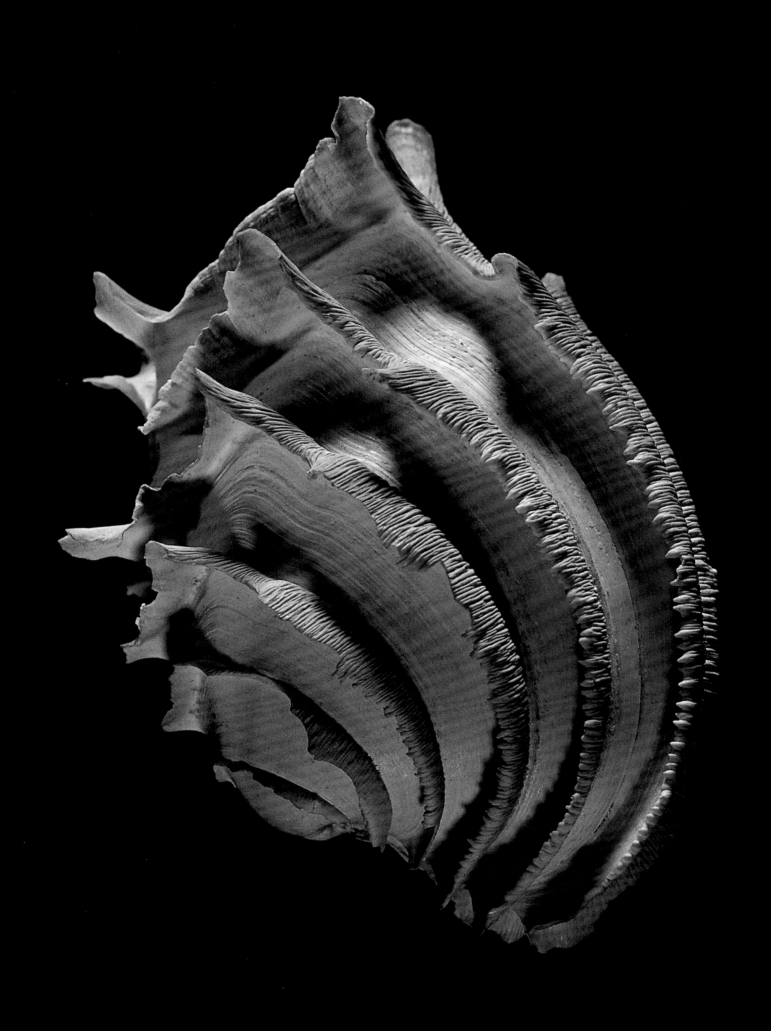

Veneridae
Chione paphia
Distribution: The Caribbean to Brazil,
in shallow water
Average size: 1.2 inches (3 cm)
Frequency: Moderately common

Veneridae
Pitar lupanaria
Distribution: From western Mexico
to Peru, on beaches in the intertidal zones
Average size: 2 inches (5 cm)
Frequency: Common
Observations: Rare to find specimens with
the long spines intact

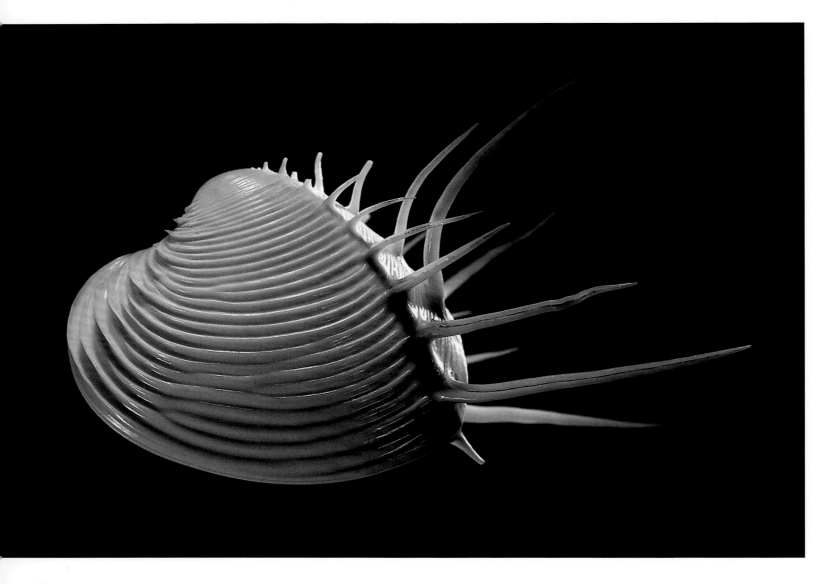

Veneridae

Bassina hiraseana

Distribution: Japan, the Kii Peninsula to the Amami Islands, on fine sand from 65–650 feet (20–200 m)

Average size: 0.8 inch (2 cm)

Frequency: Moderately common

Argonautidae
Argonauta argo
Distribution: In all warm seas
Average size: 8 inches (20 cm)
Frequency: Common in certain seasons
Observations: Pelagic (in the open sea,
away from the coast or sea floor)

▶

Argonautidae

Argonauta cornuta

Distribution: Tropical, western United States

Average size: 4 inches (10 cm)

Frequency: Locally uncommon

Observations: Pelagic (in the open sea, away from the coast or sea floor)

Argonautidae

Argonauta hians

Distribution: Atlantic Ocean and tropical Pacific

Average size: 1.2 inches (4 cm)

Frequency: Uncommon

▼

Argonautidae

Argonauta nouryi

Distribution: Baja California to Peru, on beaches, carried in by waves

Average size: 1.2 inches (4 cm)

Frequency: Uncommon

Argonautidae
Argonauta boettgeri
Distribution: Pacific Ocean and Sea of Japan
Average size: 1.2 inches (4 cm)
Frequency: Relatively rare
Observations: Epilagic (in the open sea, to
a depth of 656 feet/200 m)

Argonautidae
Argonauta nodosa
Distribution: Indo-Pacific, in
cold water
Average size: 4.7 inches (12 cm)
Frequency: Locally common

Nautilidae
Nautilus macromphalus
Distribution: New Caledonia, in
deep water
Average size: 6 inches (16 cm)
Frequency: Relatively common

▶

Nautilidae

Nautilus pompilius

Distribution: The Philippines and the
Palau islands; dead, they float everywhere
Average size: 6 inches (15 cm)
Frequency: Locally common
Observations: Live in colonies

▼

Nautilidae

Nautilus scrobiculatus

Distribution: New Guinea and the
Solomon Islands
Average size: 6.3 inches (16 cm)
Frequency: Uncommon
Observations: Has a small hole in
the first spiral

Spirulidae

Spirula spirula

Distribution: In all warm waters

Average size: 0.8 inch (2 cm)

Frequency: Frequently carried on waves, often dead

Observations: Pelagic (in the open sea, away from the coast or sea floor)

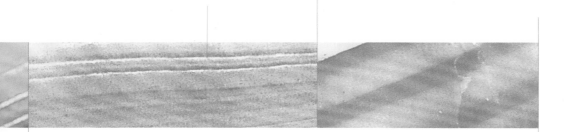

Dentaliidae
Dentalium elephantinum
Distribution: South of the Philippines
to Japan
Average size: 2.8 inches (7 cm)
Frequency: Common

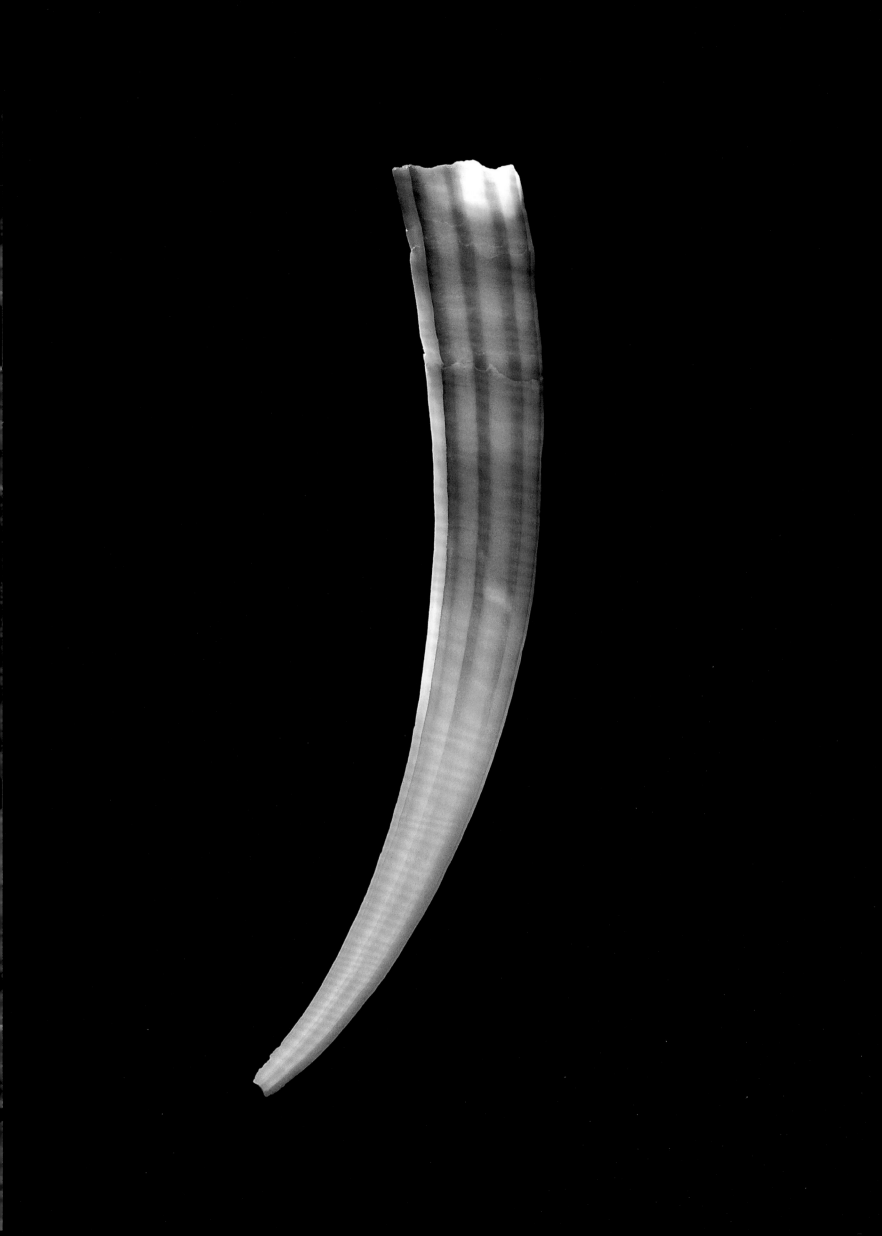

▶

Dentaliidae
Dentalium vernedei
Distribution: Eastern Asia, from depths
of 65–325 feet (20–100 m)
Average size: 5.1 inches (13 cm)
Frequency: Common

Dentaliidae
Dentalium rossati
Distribution: The Red Sea, Israel
Average size: 2.4 inches (6 cm)
Frequency: Locally common

▼

Dentaliidae
Dentalium aprinum
Distribution: Indo-Pacific
Average size: 2 inches (5 cm)
Frequency: Common
Observations: Synonymous with
Dentalium taiwanum

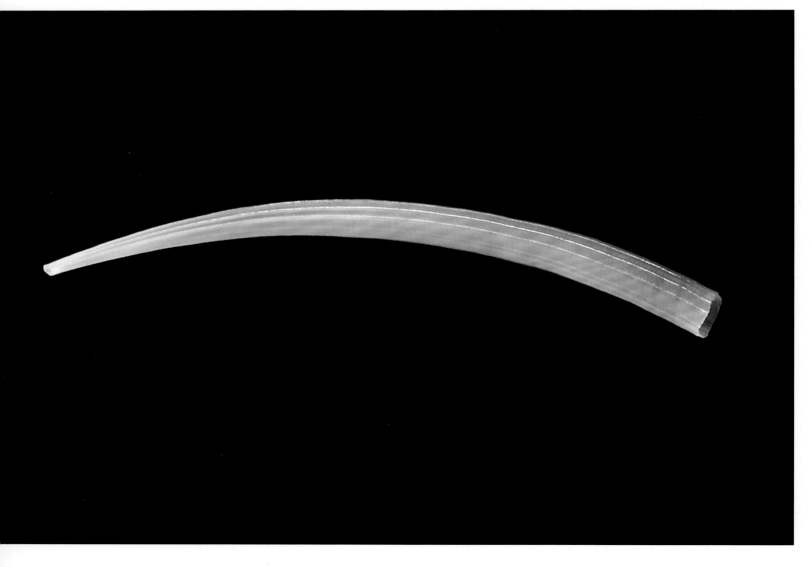

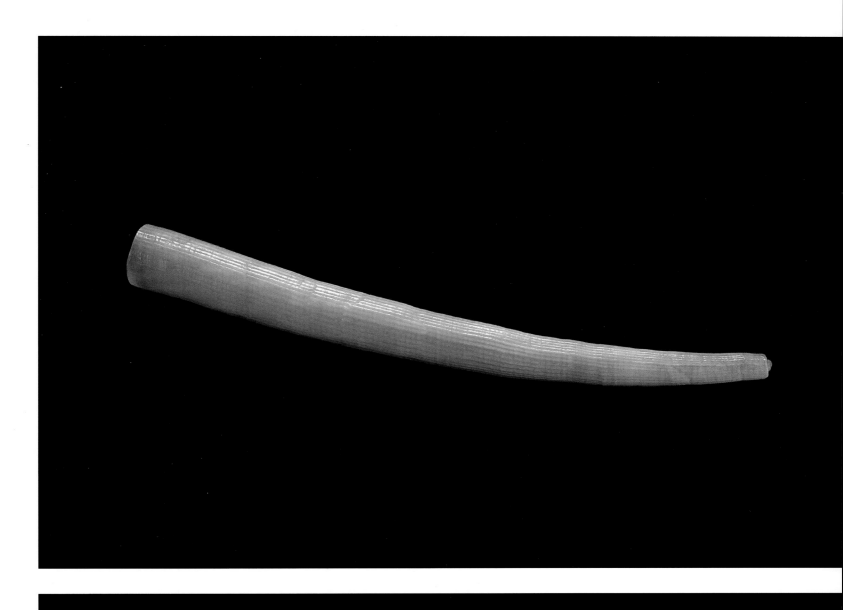

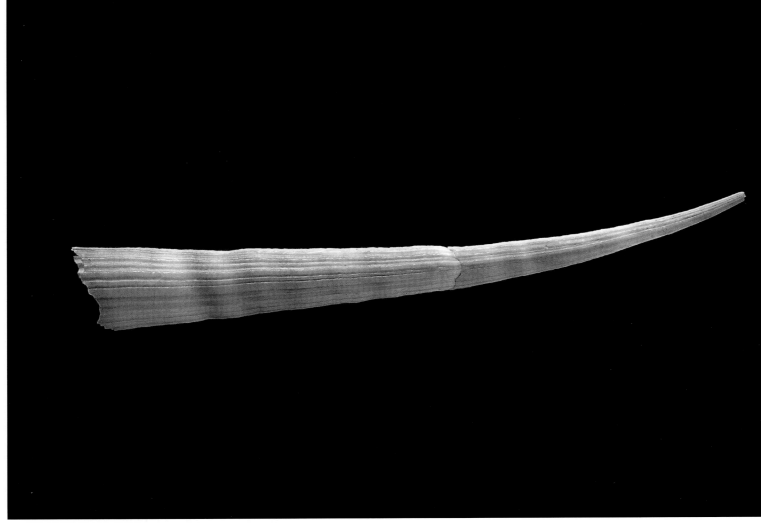

Chitonidae
Chiton squamosus
Distribution: The Caribbean
Average size: 2.8 inches (7 cm)
Frequency: Common

Ischnochitonidae
Tonicella lineata
Distribution: From Japan to Alaska
and California
Average size: 1.2 inches (4 cm)
Frequency: Common

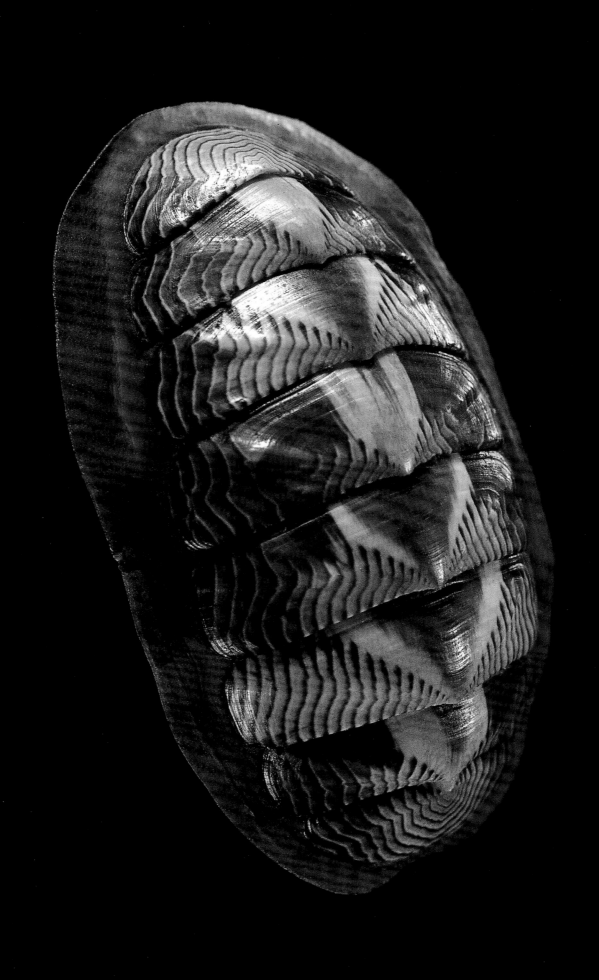

Classifications

Mollusks are subdivided into six classes: gastropods, bivalves, cephalopods, scaphopods, polyplacophorans, aplacoforans and monoplacophorans (the latter is almost totally extinct), which are in turn subdivided into numerous families. What follows is a listing of their principal characteristics and brief comments about the families that each belong to and are illustrated in this book.

Gastropods (Class Gastropoda)

The gastropods live both on land and water; some are freshwater dwellers, though the largest numbers live in marine environments. There are 60,000 to 75,000 species of gastropods alone, making them the largest class of mollusks.

The gastropod foot is well developed and extends to form a better contact with the surface of its substrate: the foot moves through a series of undulating contractions, while mucus secretions allow it to adhere to the substrate. The back of the foot is, in some cases, equipped with a horned or calcareous operculum, which serves to close the shell's opening when the animal seeks refuge inside it. The shell is formed through twisting of the visceral mass during the mollusk's development, creating a spiral form, more or less compressed according to each individual species. It is as if the mollusk has rolled up, or coiled its shell — compacting it so it is not too large — in order to transport it more effectively on its foot. This coiling activity is almost always carried out in a clockwise (right-spiraling) direction; these species are referred to as dextral. Other species are referred to as sinistral (counterclockwise coiling, or left-spiraling); although sinistral individuals sometimes occur in a species that is normally dextral. These extremely rare shells may even be the subjects of worship, such as the sinistral form of *Turbinella pyrum*, the sacred "Chank" held by the Hindu god Vishnu. There are also species in which the larva's shell is sinistral, but changes direction later in development. The number of spiral turns defines the species, from zero, as in *Patella* (a genus of limpets in which only the larval shell is spiraled) up to 50 in the auger shell *Terebra triseriata*! This twisting of the body has an effect on the internal organs — except for a single example of primitively doubled organs, the majority of gastropods have, for example, just one gill and one kidney. Their heads, not subjected to the same twisting, have two eyes and one or two pairs of tentacles.

MARINE SPECIES

Aporrhaididae

This small family, consisting of four to six species according to authorities, is related to the strombids. Even very common species like *Aporrhais pespelicanis* are rarely found in perfect condition.

Architectonicidae

These species are found in the deepest tropical and subtropical waters, feeding on coral and anemones. Due to their extended, pelagic larval stage, they are widely distributed. Much prized due to their unique design, these shells are particularly strong with a heavy spire, axial ridges and callus. This shell is also unusual by virtue of its operculum. About 90 species are known.

Buccinidae

This family consists of numerous species distributed all over the world, including all oceans, from tropical to Antarctic. They are characterized by a very thick periostracum. Species living in warm marine habitats are the most colorful, and smaller than those in more northern waters. Members of the genera *Siphonalia* and *Babylonia* are the most popular among collectors. Good quality specimens are rare. They feed primarily on dead animals as well as some bivalves and can be extremely destructive for commercial shellfish farms.

Bullidae

These herbivorous species reside on sandy bottoms in shallow, warm water amid algae. It is easy to find perfect specimens requiring no cleaning. About 25 species are known.

Campanilidae

Only one species of this family survives today, which during the Tertiary reached lengths up to 3 feet (1 m)!

Cancellariidae

The majority of the approximately 200 species in this family lives in deep waters and is uncommon or rare, and their medium-size shells are extremely varied in morphology. The *Trigonostoma* and *Cancellaria* are much prized for their beauty and variety.

Cassidae

Large in size, these animals have thick shells. They live on sand, always in shallow water, feeding on sea urchins and other small animals. Most species are tropical or subtropical and can be found in perfect condition without cleaning. Specimens with an operculum, when still intact, are very much sought after. During the 1980s, deep-living species like *Galeodea* were relatively common in northwestern Australia, but are hard to find today.

Conidae

This family, much prized among collectors, contains many species. Cones live in warm waters where they hunt worms, other mollusks and even fish. They accomplish this through a specialized organ: a long proboscis tipped with a venomous tooth (harpoon) that is very thin and barbed at the tip. The cone thrusts its proboscis forward and embeds the tooth in its prey, resulting in immediate paralysis. Although the tooth remains implanted in the victim, a new one grows in its place. The venom of some of the larger cone species can be dangerous — even deadly — to humans, as it can cause respiratory paralysis. In French Polynesia, cones cause more deaths than do shark attacks.

Coralliophilidae

The genus *Latiaxis* in this superb family contains numerous spiny species, most of which live in deep water. The shells are rarely perfect, but much appreciated by collectors, even with minor faults. There are about 250 species.

Cypraeidae

Among cowries, the lips of the mantle turn in and secrete brilliantly colored enamel, which renders these shells so valuable to collectors. This is among the most popular families because in addition to being very shiny and vividly colored, their shape ensures that they are not very fragile. (Our grandmothers used them as darning eggs.) One small species, *Cypraea moneta*, was once used as currency in India and Africa, particularly during the slave trade between northern Africa and North America. As late as the 19th century, large quantities of these shells were kept at the London Stock Exchange, but increasing volumes led to a progressive decline the value of these shells, until their cost of transport by boat or overland was no longer worth it. And that was the end of this unique form of currency.

Epitoniidae

The staircase shells, which number several hundred species, are found worldwide in deep ocean waters. They live in close proximity with Cnidaria (such as sea anemones and coral), which they feed on. These shells are unusual in that their spires are only loosely joined. One species, *Epitonium scalare*, was the most prized of shells during the 17th century. Counterfeit copies were made of rice paper for gullible collectors who went all the way to China for them.

Fasciolariidae

Many species in this family are very large, some exceeding 2 feet (60 cm) in length. They inhabit tropical and subtropical zones and many can be found in moderately deep waters. Since they are generally not brightly colored (white or brown), they require extensive cleaning, except for *Fusinus*. Since it is difficult to properly identify them because of this, there is not much interest in them among collectors.

Ficidae

These rather thin-shelled mollusks live in tropical waters, hidden in the sand on the sloping continental shelf. The shape of their spines does not vary much, but their finely textured surfaces, which differ from one species to another, make them interesting to collectors. They are nonetheless rarely found in private collections. About 20 species are known.

Haliotidae

The abalone live in the coastal regions of all oceans, just above the tidal margins. Stuck to rocks, they travel at night in search of algae as their main food source. In its outermost whorl, the shell is pierced with holes; sensory tentacles will exit some of these holes, while others will serve as the entry and exit points of water required for respiration. As the shell grows, new holes are formed while older ones become plugged. The result is a constant number of open holes in the species. These animals are also harvested for food, though their beautiful mother-of-pearl has long been used to make buttons for luxury clothing.

Harpidae

Containing only about 40 species, harp shells are carnivorous and live on the sandy beds of tropical seas. They have the ability to voluntarily shed a part of their foot to escape predators. Some of the most beautiful shells in existence can be found in the Harpidae family; the vivid colors and their numerous well-marked ribs account for their attractiveness. The most prized is *Harpa costata*, which has twice as many ribs as other species in the genus. It is endemic to Mauritius. Certain harp shells with little coloring (though not albinos) are fished in the Maldives and the Indian Ocean.

Hydatinidae

These residents of warm seas, which gather their nourishment from marine worms, have very thin shells. They are often found on the beach, carried by wave activity once they are empty. Their transverse-colored bands are fragile and disappear slowly with exposure to light. They must therefore be preserved in a dark drawer rather than displayed in a window.

Littorinidae

The littorinids could almost be classified as amphibians. They live on rocky areas in tidal zones normally uncovered by waves. Thanks to an operculum that hermetically closes the shell, and behind which they maintain a certain degree of moisture, they have a great resistance to drying out. The Littorinidae feed on algae, which is locally abundant, often on the branches of mangroves that populate their habitats.

Marginellidae

In these animals, the mantle may entirely cover the shell. They are all predators living principally in warm seas, but also in more temperate waters.

Mitridae

The miters live mainly in sandy depths, beneath coral or rocks in warm seas. Their horn is particularly well developed and they feed on worms. Certain species secrete a purple liquid when they are disturbed.

Costellariidae

This family is quite close to that of the Mitridae, whose large colorful species have always been prized. Some, like *Vexillum stainforthi* and *Vexillum dennison,* are quite well known.

Muricidae

The murexes are characterized by having an extremely sculpted shell, though quite lacking in pattern. These mollusks are predators that prefer warm, shallow waters. Known to humans for more than 3,500 years, purple dye was extracted from the bodies of a Mediterranean murex species. A large number of individuals were required to fabricate the dye and the process was quite complicated. A host of difficulties meant that only quite valuable fabrics were colored with the purple dye, and they remained the reserve of kings or nobility and, later on, church dignitaries.

Neritidae

Whether they live in fresh, brackish or salty water, the hundreds of species of neritids are tropical. Although shell ornamentation is unremarkable in these mollusks, they make it up in their coloration, which is often stunning and quite varied, even on the interior.

Neritopsidae

Very similar to the Neritidae, they differ in the presence of a thick, white operculum (in the Neritidae it is brown and thin).

Olividae

Tropical mollusks, olive shells remain buried in the sand during the daytime and move around at night to feed on worms, other mollusks or carrion. They capture their prey, detected at a distance, and pull it into the soil with their extremely enlarged foot. Olives are capable of stocking many microscopic organisms in a fold of their mantle, in order to pass them down to their stomach later.

Ovulidae

These mollusks, close to the porcelains, do not share their brilliance and are generally of small stature. They live among coral, and have "borrowed" their coloration and appearance. Their unusual form and vibrant colors make them quite appreciated by collectors.

Personidae

The *Distorsio* genus was once placed in the Ranellidae family, then in the Cymatiidae. Living in quite deep water, they are often quite rare. They have a very irregular opening partially obstructed by a fold in the columella (the shell's axis). Their yellow-brown operculum is chitinous.

Phasianellidae

This is a small family containing magnificent, brilliant shells with weak structure, but varied colors and designs. They are found in Australia, Japan and South Africa. Relatively common, they are much appreciated by collectors.

Pleurotomariidae

This family is prized by collectors, and the value of certain shells is quite high. These mollusks escaped the cataclysm that destroyed the dinosaurs. They display a slit on their last whorl; it is through this opening that their waste products are evacuated. As the shell grows, this slit is plugged. The pleurotomariids live in deep water colonized by algae and feed on sponges. Some can be observed and collected only with the help of small scientific submarines — a costly endeavor to the amateur malacologist. Other species remain happily accessible to less well-off collectors.

Ranellidae

Related to the Bursidae, these were originally called Cymatiidae. These shallow-water mollusks are predators that produce venomous saliva. The periostracum is important in camouflage and collectors are advised to keep at least one specimen with an intact periostracum. The conches of larger species have been used as sounding horns.

Siliquariidae

This family, consisting of approximately 20 species, lives inside sponges in deep tropical waters. The long spire on these shells grows in a very irregular manner and its whorls are not joined, making it difficult to obtain intact specimens.

Strombidae

This semiprecious family is one of the most popular and does not contain any small shells. Some Strombidae are quite famous. For example, only one specimen of *Strombus listeri* was known to exist for nearly 300 years, and its habitat (Thailand) was only discovered in the 1970s; another species, *S. oldi*, was rediscovered during the early 1980s in Somalia. Today, the small *S. scalariformis* from the Philippines is the most coveted. The Strombidae are herbivores and live in colonies. The operculum is too straight to close the shell off, but its extended shape provides some defense, and its sickle-like siphonal canal is used for leaping movement. These are very active animals and extremely mobile.

Terebridae

These shells are invariably thin and pointed, with lengths varying from 0.6 inch (1.5 cm) to more than 8 inches (20 cm). Their sculpture and patterns are also quite diverse, which is what makes them so attractive. They reside below the surface of the sand in shallow tropical waters, and are carnivorous, with some species also being venomous.

Turritellidae

Since they generally live in shallow water under muddy soil, members of this family feed on detritus by scooping it up onto sticky mucus. These are large, beautiful shells with a chitinous operculum.

Tonnidae

This family of less than 30 species has rather thin, fragile shells that are globular in shape. They are generally not much sought after by collectors — they are too bulky and difficult to evaluate as they are all similar in shape. These mollusks secrete an acidic saliva which can paralyze their prey.

Calliostomatidae

This recently established family contains some 60 species, all previously classified in the Trochidae family. Though small in size (0.6–1 inch/1.5–2.5 cm), these magnificent shells are much coveted for their varied colors as well as their extremely delicate markings. They are found almost everywhere in tropical and polar latitudes, from intertidal zones to deep water, and on varied substrates, including rocks, coral reefs and debris.

Trochidae

The majority of trochids are herbivorous and live on rocks where algae grow. It is a very interesting family in the diversity of its superb shells. It encompasses a large number of species, and several have been used for their mother-of-pearl in button-making and the decoration of objects, such as small items of furniture.

Turbinellidae

The majority of species in this family feed on worms and bivalves in the low waters of shorelines. Their chitinous operculum has a fistlike shape. Their eggs are deposited in a circle, in horned capsules.

Turbidinae

Turbidins live on the high bottoms of tropical and subtropical coral reefs. They are prized by collectors. Several require substantial cleaning. Their calcareous operculums are thick, with varied forms and designs. That of *Turbo petholatus* is extremely decorated and very colored; named "cat's eye," it is used in jewelry, notably earrings, once very much appreciated by fishermen's wives. The sinistral (left-spiraling) form of *Turbinella pyrum* is the sacred "Chank " of Hinduism.

Turridae

This is the most numerous family of the gastropods; there are several thousand species distributed through a large quantity of genera. They are to be found in all seas, from shallow to great depths, on continental shelves. Many are known by a single unique example. These mollusks have a slit on their last whorl, used for water exchange and waste evacuation. All make venom.

Volutidae

Spending much of the time buried in sand, volutes escape during the night to feed. They surround their prey with their large foot while paralyzing it with their saliva. The reproductive cycle of these mollusks does not have a swimming larval stage — the eggs develop straight into tiny volutes. Each species does not spread itself very far, with many among them having a reduced distribution restrained to one island or even one beach. Within the species, certain colorations are specific to one population, and passionate collectors are able to identify the precise origin of one volute solely by its design and colors. This family has long been known as "the family of millionaires."

TERRESTRIAL SPECIES

Ariophantidae

This is a fairly important family of terrestrial gastropods, with the most prized species originating in Indonesia. Thanks to a fine periostracum, their colors are completely different depending on whether they are found in the rainy or the dry season.

Bradybaenidae

The bradybaenids comprise one of the largest families of terrestrial mollusks, with representatives found in all global regions.

Camaenidae

The animals are spread throughout subtropical and tropical regions, notably in Brazil, Japan and the Philippines.

Cyclophoridae

These have a widespread distribution similar to the Camaenidae.

Helminthoglyptidae

Magnificently colored, the best known species is *Polymita picta*, found exclusively in the east of Cuba. Once very widespread, it is now rare due to the use of agricultural insecticides.

Odontostomidae

These are found exclusively in the New World: Argentina, Brazil and Uruguay

Orthalicidae

These are only seen in the tropical Americas: the Caribbean, Panama and Peru.

Pomatiasidae

The Pomatiasidae are found in northern Africa (Morocco) as well as in Europe on Malta, and in France, Greece and Portugal.

Bivalves (Class Bivalvia)

Ranked second in the number of species (about 30,000), bivalves are exclusively aquatic mollusks. Their name is derived from the way that their shells consist of two halves, though there are alternative common names given to the class based on other characteristics. For example, the name Lamellibranchiae has been used due to the morphology of their gills in the form of lamellae. These lamellae are covered with vibrating cilia that have two functions: first, to flush water in and out for oxygen take-up and the disposal of waste products, and second, to act as filters for nutrients and send them toward the mouth. This mouth, which lacks a radula, is all that remains of the heads of these animals and is the reason they are also known as "acephalopods."

The "iron grip" foot of bivalves allows them to crawl and sometimes "jump" on underwater surfaces, but mainly it is used to bury themselves in the substrate. Although underwater substrates are usually loose, some bivalve species can burrow into wood and even rock, if necessary. The bivalve foot also contains a special gland that secretes a thread of silky material after it is nestled in a groove; this material subsequently solidifies to "glue" the bivalve to the substrate, creating what is known as a byssus. The animal then continues to produce additional filaments to firmly anchor it in place. (In history, the Romans used the byssus from a very large bivalve species, *Pinna nobilis*, which used to inhabit the Mediterranean, for weaving. The demand for this precious fabric ended after the Second World War, thereby preserving these animals.)

The byssus "anchor" is not always permanent, however — some species can break free and move to another location. Other species, though, become permanently sessile once implanted, as one of their shell halves is also connected to the substrate and a second group of filaments effectively forms a lid over it. These species (oysters are a good example) have also lost their now vestigial foot.

Whether free-living or sessile, the bivalve's shell has a protective function and totally encapsulates its occupant in case of danger. For this reason, the two half-shells, or valves, are hinged via elastic filaments that help keep them in an open position, while two large, internal muscles contract to close the shell when needed. To complete the mechanism, the space between the two valves contains smoothly overlapping teeth and ridges, creating a life-saving seal.

Arcidae

This is a common family of shells. Their thick periostracum makes them difficult to clean. Several small species live on the shelf of continental plateaus. They are largely used as a food source, along with other seafoods.

Cardiidae

The long foot of these shells enables them to move by small "steps." These mollusks live buried just under the surface of the soil.

Glossidae

These are spherical shells which, when viewed in profile, look like a stylized heart. The best known are named *Glossus humanus* ("human heart").

Pectinidae

The scallop's mantle edge is equipped with fine, tiny tentacles as well as small, beautiful, simple eyes, which only enable the animal to distinguish variations in movement and light intensity. In these mollusks, young individuals live attached to the substrate by their byssus, whereas older scallops are free living, more or less buried in the sand, and capable of reactive swimming.

Pholadidae

These rock-piercing mollusks drill burrows, with the shell slowly "eating away" at the rock. The hollow thus formed can be long and become enlarged as it deepens. Eventually, the animal can no longer escape from its burrow as it becomes larger than the entry point. Pholadidae have luminescent mucus.

Spondylidae

This bivalve family is prized by collectors — with their pleasing size, vivid coloration and several spines, these are true jewels. However, cleaning them requires a lot of work. These animals often make agglomerates of several shells. In species living in loose soil, the inferior valve is equipped with large spines, which enable them to become anchored.

Tridacnidae

It is within this family that one finds the larges bivalves: the shell of a giant clam (*Tridacna gigas*) can measure up to 5 feet (1.5 m) in diameter and weigh more than 450 pounds (200 kg)! This animal poses a danger to divers if their hands or feet become lodged between the two valves. Tridacnids live mainly on massive coral, which they adhere solidly to with their byssus, eventually becoming encrusted on the surface of the coral. They live in association with unicellular algae, lodged in the lip of their very dilated mantles. This fold stretches to the point of containing small transparent organisms, in the shape of lenses, to capture light.

Veneridae

This is the largest bivalve family. They are abundantly fished, principally by dragging in the open oceans. The shells gathered in warmer waters are the most colorful.

Cephalopods (Class Cephalopoda)

Not as numerous as other classes, with some 700 species, cephalopods were dominant several hundred million years ago, along with the ammonites, which became extinct about the same time as the dinosaurs. Despite their antiquity, cephalopods are among the most advanced mollusks. They possess highly developed nervous systems and complex behavior not found among other invertebrates, and their eyesight is comparable to that of vertebrates. The cephalopod foot is directly linked to the head (hence their name) and is partitioned into several tentacles surrounding the mouth. These tentacles are usually covered with suction pads that serve to capture and hold prey for these carnivorous mollusks. Some species also secrete a potent venom, and because of this their bites can be deadly to humans. Generally, though, cephalopods are not aggressive and usually try to swim away when threatened or disturbed, releasing a cloud of ink as they flee. They are also capable of rapidly changing their skin coloration to match their immediate surroundings.

Despite all this, these animals are not of great interest to shell collectors. Their shells are most often internal or totally absent, and only the handful of species of the genus *Nautilus* have the external shells typically associated with mollusks. Though not very thick, these shells are pearl-like, and this characteristic was very much appreciated by prisoners on Devil's Island, who were allowed to carve *Nautilus* shells as a reward for good behavior. Many of these carvings were remarkably good and prized as works of art.

Argonautidae

The argonaut's shell is not fixed to its body; the animal must hold onto it with its small tentacles. It is with two of these specialized arms that the female makes the eggcase "shell" that will hold her eggs as well as parts of her body. The six other arms serve as oars. These animals live in open waters and never venture to the bottom. Males are 20 times smaller than females. During reproduction, part of one of the male's tentacles loses its suckers and becomes detached in order to fertilize a female with the sperm he carries. Once the young argonauts leave the eggcase, it is abandoned by the female and can be found empty, deposited on beaches by wave activity.

Nautilidae

The nautilus shell is comprised of a series of chambers that are progressively sealed as the animal grows; the nautilus occupies the last — and largest — of these chambers. The walls that divide the chambers are pierced, enabling a duct, known as the siphuncle, to traverse them — the only connection the nautilus has to its former living chambers. By varying the amount of gas (nitrogen) contained in the shell, the nautilus can ascend or descend to different depths. These animals are equipped with a large number of sucker-free tentacles and their eyes do not contain a solid lens.

Spirulidae

In spirulids, the mantle almost entirely covers the shell, which is chambered and traversed with a siphuncle — similar to the nautili. These small mollusks possess eight arms and two longer tentacles with suckers. Very common, they are present in all warm waters to depths of 3,000 feet (920 m). Their empty shells float to the surface, and can be found on beaches, on the sand and in algae brought in by wave activity.

Scaphopods (Class Scaphopoda)

The scaphopods comprise a homogenous class of marine mollusks; its shape is reminiscent of an elephant tusk with two large openings. The larger of the two orifices contains a tubelike foot that can stretch and enlarge enormously and dig into the mud or sand while remaining firmly anchored to the animal's shell. These animals are also found buried in the sea floor at water depths of 16,000 feet (5,000 m); here they capture and feed on plankton and microscopic algae using long, thin tentacles that are covered with mucus-emitting glands to help bring food to their mouths. The other opening is buried in the sea floor and used to release waste products, eggs and sperm, as well as take in water for respiration. These mollusks do not have gills, however — this function is served by the mantle instead.

There are about 400 known species of scaphopods, some of which were used as currency by Native Americans, and they are still sometimes used as ornamental jewelry.

Polyplacophorans (Class Polyplacophora)

Also known as chitins, polyplacophorans live mostly under rocks in the intertidal zone, but can also be found at depths up to 13,000 feet (4,000 m). Their shells are covered with eight articulated and overlapping plates. Although they do not have eyes on their heads, the plates are covered with many photoreceptors linked directly to olfactory and tactile organs. The portion of the mantle closest to the shell is folded out, covered with pointed spines, hairs or bristles, and covers an internal cavity holding as many as 75 pairs of gills.

These mollusks resemble woodlice and, similarly, can roll themselves into a ball for protection if they are turned on their backs. They spend their time grazing on algae while remaining solidly anchored to the sea floor with their large foot. The radula is covered with an iron-rich mineral, which allows them to graze on calcified algae forms. These mollusks move extremely slowly (much slower than a snail) and, to no surprise, only a few of the 900 known species are carnivorous. It is not surprising, then, that they hunt while laying in wait.

A biologist by training and a naturalist at heart, **Paul Starosta** has worked as a professional photographer for more than 20 years. He has published over 30 books on plants and animals, and has won several awards.

Jacques Senders, accompanied by his wife, Rita, devotes a major portion of his time to deep-sea diving and the harvesting of shells. Their collection is based on aesthetics, as well as the quality of harvested specimens. Jacques Senders has served as the vice-president of the Société Belge de Malacologie for many years. In addition to writing articles about his trips and the study of mollusks, he is the author of several books. Some shell species have been named *sendersi* in his honor.

Acknowledgments

Paul Starosta wishes to thank Micheline Cellier and Évelyne Jouve for their valued help, and for their kindness in making themselves available.

A Firefly Book

Published by Firefly Books Ltd. 2007

English translation © 2007 Firefly Books

First printing

Publisher Cataloging-in-Publication Data (U.S.)
Starosta, Paul.
    Shells / Paul Starosta ; Jacques Senders ; Paolo Portoghesi.
[384] p. : col. photos. ; cm.
Includes index.
ISBN-13: 978-1-55407-321-4
ISBN-10: 1-55407-321-9
1. Shells. 2. Shells – Pictorial works. 3. Mollusks. 4. Shells in art.
I. Senders, Jacques. II. Portoghesi, Paolo. III. Title.
594 dc22   QL405.S737   2007

Library and Archives Canada Cataloguing in Publication
Starosta, Paul
    Shells / Paul Starosta, Jacques Senders, Paolo Portoghesi.
Includes index.
ISBN-13: 978-1-55407-321-4
ISBN-10: 1-55407-321-9
    1. Shells. 2. Mollusks. 3. Shells–Pictorial works.
4. Mollusks–Collectors and collecting. 5. Shells in art.
I. Portoghesi, Paolo II. Senders, J. (Jacques) III. Title.
QL403.S72 2007   594   C2007-902636-2

Published in the United States by
Firefly Books (U.S.) Inc.
P.O. Box 1338, Ellicott Station
Buffalo, New York 14205

Published in Canada by
Firefly Books Ltd.
66 Leek Crescent
Richmond Hill, Ontario L4B 1H1

Original title: *Conchiglie*
ISBN : 978-88-6034-008-5

Colour separation: AG Media SRL, Milan

Printed in July 2007 by Conti Tipocolor in Calenzano, Florence

Printed in Italy

CREDITS

Editorial Coordinator: Laura Maggioni
Creative Director: Lara Gariboldi
Page Production: Annarita de Sanctis
English translation: Margaret and Klaus Brasch

Text authors: Paul Starosta, Jacques Senders, Paolo Portoghesi

Photography: Paul Starosta

© Equatore, Milan, 2007

© Rights Reserved: pp. 8, 9, 11, 12, 14, 15 bottom, 16.
© Rights Reserved: page 10 Emilio Terry by SIAE 2007.
© Archivio Alinari: page 13.
© Rights Reserved: page 15 top – Jørn Utzon by SIAE 2007.

The publisher retains the rights to all illustrations not individually credited.

Page 7: Aristotle. *The History of Animals*, translated by D'Arcy Wentworth Thompson. eBooks @ Adelaide, 2004. http://etext.library.adelaide.edu.au/a/aristotle/history.

Page 29: R.L. Herbert. *Nature's Workshop: Renoir's Writings on the Decorative Arts.* Yale University Press: New Haven, 2000.

PHOTO CAPTIONS

Cover
Trochidae
Clanculus pharaonius
Distribution: Indian Ocean, under rocks in the intertidal zone
Average size: 0.8 inches (2 cm)
Frequency: Locally common

page 2
Glossidae
Meiocardia moltkiana
Distribution: Eastern India, in shallow waters
Average size: 1.2 inches (3 cm)
Frequency: Uncommon

page 4
Arcidae
Anadara sp.
Distribution: Indo-Pacific
Average size: 1.2 inches (4 cm)
Frequency: Common

page 6
Muricidae
Thais cingulata
Distribution: South Africa
Average size: 1.2 inches (3 cm)
Frequency: Locally common
Observation: Synonymous with *Nucella cingulata*

page 18
Cardiidae
Ctenocardia victor
Distribution: Western Pacific Ocean, widely distributed to depths of 325 feet (100 m)
Average size: 1 inch (2.5 cm)
Frequency: Uncommon

page 366
Muricidae
Murex elongata
Distribution: Southwest Japan
Average size: 2.8 inches (7 cm)
Frequency: Common in Japan, but quite rare in the Philippines
Observation: Synonymous with *Murex clavus*